Choose Words
Choose Life
51 Dates That Change Lives

Elissa,
Pga 34:8
Blessings!
Lynelle

LynelleZandstra

ISBN: 9780982666531
RELIGION / CHRISTIAN EDUCATION / CHILDREN & YOUTH

Published by Pilot Communications Group
www.BookRipple.com

HOW TO REACH LYNELLE ZANDSTRA:
www.lynellezandstra.com

HOW TO ORDER:
www.lynellezandstra.com

"Treat your children as if
you won't have them tomorrow.
Train them as if they won't
have you tomorrow."
— Dave Jones

Dedication

To Mario, the most amazing friend, husband and fellow sojourner a woman could ask for. You made the journey possible.

To Laura, Will, Joel, MaryClaire, Hannah, Daniel, and Sarah Grace, the most amazing children a mom could ever ask for. You made the journey joyful.

To HIM who made the journey. Soli Deo Gloria.

"I've a feeling we're not in
Kansas any more."
— Dorothy, from *The Wizard of Oz*

Contents

Introduction

I can remember the moment as if it were yesterday. It was the moment that I held my amazingly beautiful, firstborn daughter, Laura. It was a moment of absolute joy and stark and utter terror.

I realized then that I was totally and completely unprepared for this new season and journey called parenthood. That realization was the beginning of what has become a 25-year search to figure out how to "do this right." All I knew was that it was a totally different world than the one in which I grew up and that it would require a totally different parenting paradigm.

Two years later, God was to begin to answer all of my questions at an incredible place called Pine Cove. We spent the next 12 years attending a week of family camp each summer. We went back every chance we got. Slowly, God began to completely rewrite my definition of family and to give me a vision for what it was even supposed to look like. For 12 years as campers, and now starting our 13th year on staff there, I have been privileged to hear the absolute best teaching available on parenting, marriage, and authentic Biblical living. I am forever indebted to all of the fabulous speakers who, through the investment of their lives there, forever changed my life, my family, and my legacy.

The very first summer we attended, our speaker was Tim Kimmel. He turned everything I mistakenly thought I knew about parenting upside down and inside out. Talk about challenging! Almost everything I know about parenting is a direct effect of his teaching. The basic precepts of parenting for purpose instead of for quiet, the difference between punishment and discipline, the principles of intentionality and deliberateness — all of these I learned from him. Tim Kimmel, John Trent, Mark Bailey, Jerry Bridges and many, many others: these are the giants of the faith and the defenders of the family under whose teaching I have been privileged to sit.

But for a generation my age and younger, the question was, "How do I make this real?" When you haven't grown up this way, the ability to take these truths and put them into words that make sense to a five year old or even a fifteen year old is a daunting prospect.

There were times when I spent months begging God to show me how to speak in a way that my kids could hear and comprehend. "How exactly do I explain this to my kids?" was a question I was regularly asked when I spoke to young mothers at retreats or conferences. "I need a script and specific ideas," was a constant request.

This book is my attempt to meet that very specific, very real need. These are the conversations I had with my children as I attempted to explain, on their level of understanding and comprehension, challenging concepts like the sovereignty of God, suffering, and sanctification.

I would be incredibly remiss not to thank the many people who made this possible. First and foremost, thank you to the most incredible husband ever, Mario. You have nurtured, shepherded, and loved me faithfully and fabulously. I love you. To my seven patient, joyful, wonderful children. You were the reason for the journey. I love you to the moon and back, no take aways! Specifically, to my eldest, Laura Zandstra Murray, who typed the original manuscript of this for me after discovering that I had actually written it on yellow legal pads. To Wendy Baker, who read and reread, analyzed and critiqued, thank you, thank you, thank you. To Laura Watson, who challenged me again and again (I am a slow learner) to slow down and bask in His presence. To Kathy Bosley, who prayed, called to check on me, then prayed some more. To Jennifer Woolsey, who spent countless hours welcoming my youngest ones into her family and loving them with reckless abandon. To the amazing women in my Thursday morning Bible study: Julie, Jill, Sandra, Caelin, Kaye, Marilyn and Susan; what a privilege it has been to share our hearts and our lives.

To God be the glory,

Lynelle

Chapter One

Score: Mountain Lion 1, Kitten 0

It was a gorgeous spring day. White fluffy clouds danced across a deep blue sky and an orchestra of birds sang a symphony just for us. Our family had moved just weeks before from a huge metropolitan area to the Piney Woods of East Texas. We had gone from houses that were one driveway's width apart to the middle of 750 acres of a pine tree forest.

Our children, in their own words, had "moved to heaven on earth." It was safe. Secure. Peaceful. It was the kind of place where people want to raise their children. All was well.

The calls started coming about three weeks later. Small dogs and cats were disappearing from a nearby residential area. The disappearances continued every other night or so for a few weeks. Heart-broken pet owners and their neighbors wondered aloud about the cause of this mysterious phenomenon. It didn't take long until the cause was revealed. A woman in the area, responding to her barking dog's plea to go outside, flung open the sliding glass door to her deck. Imagine her horror and surprise upon finding herself face to face with a full-grown male mountain lion. Mystery solved! Now we knew why the aforementioned small dogs and cats had been disappearing.

The neighborhood went into a sort of "pet lock-down" for the next few weeks as area officials tried unsuccessfully to trap the carnivorous newcomer. At our house, a full-scale investigation was launched into the habits and habitats of a mountain lion by my 8- and 10-year-old sons. I learned more about mountain lions than I ever wanted to know. Like the fact that they are nocturnal and will roam 25 miles in search of prey. I learned their preferred diet (small dogs, cats, and anything else they can catch!) and that mountain lions are, indeed, indigenous to this part of the country (surprise!).

But as we watched with interest the search for the ever-elusive mountain lion, it had no personal affect on us at all. We lived 15 minutes away from all the activity, and across two fairly large highways. Although it was a great source of nature study for my boys and of dinner table conversation for our family, it neither affected our lives nor changed the way we did anything.

That is, until one week later. My daughter called her beloved kitten all day long, but it never came running eagerly like it had every time before. For three days we called "Tiger" and searched the surrounding area to no avail. On the fourth day, my boys came roaring, wide-eyed and out of breath, into the house.

"Mom, we were out hiking and we found Tiger!" they shouted.

Delighted, I responded, "Thanks, boys! Your little sister will be so pleased!"

With a downcast look, Will, the eldest, replied, "No, I don't think so, Mom. We followed huge tracks down the sandy path to the pond. When we got there we found a big scuffed up area where there had been some sort of a fight, and in the middle of that area, we found this. It's all that's left, Mom." And with that, he pulled the last two inches of our kitten's tail out of his pocket. We all stared in horror at the evidence of the mountain lion's carnage.

I knew there was a mountain lion out there on the loose. But it was too far away, too removed, too isolated, to affect me personally. It was someone else's problem. Until it was too late.

I sacrificed our kitten by my presumed assumption that we were safe and secure. By not taking deliberate steps to protect it, I made it easy prey for the lion.

There is a roaring lion that desires to devour our children - the children of sweet, well-meaning Christian homes. And, unless we take deliberate, intentional steps to prepare and protect them, we make them easier game for him. I Peter 5:8 warns us: *"Be self-controlled and alert. Your enemy the devil prowls around like a roaring lion looking for someone to devour."* He's not "out there," so far away in age or distance as to be someone else's problem.

The goal of this book is to examine some very specific things that we can do in the lives of our children to teach them truths — truths that transform. It's not enough to simply *protect* our kids. A sapling must be protected until it's strong enough to be transplanted outside in a garden. Eventually, that sapling must be moved outside or it will become root bound and die. It would be a foolish gardener who would move the sapling outside without first making sure he had done everything to get the tree ready for the "outside" world.

Protecting is appropriate for a season; then we must begin to prepare them to be strong and thrive.

So it is with our children. Protecting is appropriate for a season; then we must begin to *prepare* them to be strong and thrive. The wind that would destroy a sapling causes the young tree to grow deeper roots and stronger limbs. A failure to expose and equip our kids only makes them "safe" in the sense that our kitten was "safe." It just meant we weren't really dealing with the danger.

How do we begin to prepare our children? What we want for them is a total paradigm shift, a different perspective from what the world offers. Let's look at why.

Chapter Two

Our Hearts Are Restless

Why do we need a different perspective? You can go to almost any playground or lunchroom in America and see it in action. It's called the "pecking order" pyramid. This pyramid creates a constant probing question: "Why do you deserve to be recognized or included?" If you're anywhere near my age, you probably remember the popular TV commercial jingle that sang, "My dog's better than your dog. My dog's better than yours. My dog's better 'cause he eats_____ (fill in the name of the dog food company that I do not wish to offend). My dog's better than yours!"

Of course, the thing that made the commercial so cute was the adorable pre-school boy who unashamedly boasted of loving his "better" dog above all others. From toddler-hood on, we're told, "it's just a kid thing," "all kids do it," and "it's normal." That may be true, but does that make it good? The logic that follows would be, "One million flies must be right. Trash tastes good." I don't think so.

When we first moved to the country, we decided to try (heavy emphasis on the word *try*) to raise chickens. We built them a magnificent chicken coop. We gave them absolutely everything they needed: fresh water, organic corn, and nice shade. They wanted for nothing! Imagine our horror when we emerged a few mornings later to find that the bigger chickens had ganged up on the smallest, weakest chicken and literally pecked him to death!

Assuming that he must have been a sickly chicken and that all would progress smoothly from here on, we had a respectful chicken burial service and went back to work. Our respect for successful chicken farmers rose immensely when we discovered the second victim the very next week. Once again, the bigger chickens ganged up on the next weakest one and pecked him to death. That's where we get the term "pecking order."

It's in those lunchrooms and on those playgrounds.

"My dad's bigger than your dad."

"My mom's prettier than yours."

"I'm smarter than you."

"We have more money than you."

Kids tend to judge each other based on looks, athletic abilities, money, and brains. No one is immune. The cry of every child's heart is to be part of things, to be included, to be loved; they yearn to discover "Who am I?" Our goal as parents is to move them from "*who* am I?" to "*whose* am I?" Do you hear the slight, but life-changing difference?

Have you ever had someone comment on how well behaved your children were in some public place? It feels great, doesn't it? Have you ever wanted to crawl behind the nearest potted plant when one of your children says or does something incredibly embarrassing to you? Our kids' behavior screams "success" or "failure," in reference to our ability as parents. It points its bony, accusatory finger directly at *us*. It's easy to see why we can get so caught up in their behavior. Do they obey? Do they say, "Yes, ma'am" and "No, sir." Are they obedient? Behavior is important in so far as it shows where someone's heart is. But it's not about behavior at all.

Ultimately, all behavior is an issue of the heart. I Samuel 16:7 says: "*The Lord does not look at things man looks at. Man looks at the outward appearance, but the Lord looks at the heart.*" The behavior is just a symptom of what is in the heart. Why? Because all behavior starts in the heart. It's the key issue in our parenting. Proverbs 4:23 says, "*Above all else, guard your heart. For it is the wellspring of life.*"

So how do we help our children guard their hearts? And what are we guarding them from? Even more importantly, what are we guarding them *for*? Yes, we have been saved *from* ourselves and *from* the consequences of our sin — eternal separation from God. We have also been saved *for* a lifetime of seeking and serving Him. As John Piper says, we "glorify God by enjoying Him forever."

The problem is the tyranny of the physical. How do we help our children take their eyes off of the urgent and put them on the eternal? II Corinthians 4:18 says, *"So we fix our eyes not on what is seen, but on what is unseen. For what is seen is temporary, but what is unseen is eternal."* Try telling your teenager that popularity and friends are temporary. Or, try telling your grade school-aged child that his bike and baseball will soon be ancient history. You may find yourself being met with stone-faced disbelief and resistance! The question is this: How do we teach our children what lasts, what matters, and what counts for all of eternity?

Behavior is important in so far as it shows where someone's heart is ... but it's not about behavior at all.

You're probably sitting in a chair or on a couch as you read this. Reach back and feel it. Is it real? Can you touch it? Certainly! Now reach your hand out and feel the air in front of you. Can you touch it? No. Is it real? Absolutely. Which do you need more, the chair you can feel or the air you breathe?

It proves a great point doesn't it? The "seen" screams for our attention, while the *"unseen"* is what we most desperately need. It's not an issue of learning the right techniques and thereby guaranteeing successful, happy children. It's a matter of reaching and training their hearts. It's a matter of that previously mentioned total paradigm shift, of offering them a different perspective from what the world offers. It's trading in the seen for the unseen. Let's look at how.

Chapter Three

Why Dates?

I was walking. And sweating. And doing a lot of groaning. Forty-two weeks pregnant (yes, you read that correctly). My husband, Mario, and I were obeying doctor's orders and were out on our nightly one-mile walk. A snail's paced, joint-jarring, belly-aching trudge would be a more accurate description.

As we rounded the corner, we saw them: the cute, 90-something, grey-haired couple moving equally as slowly as we were. It was a toss-up as to who was moving more precariously — me holding my belly, or the little old man holding his back. As we passed, he greeted us with, "How poignant. You're walking for a healthy beginning of a life and I'm walking for a healthy ending of a life." As the couple walked on, the old man added, "Enjoy every minute of it. Time flies and that baby will be grown and gone before you know it."

After a polite smile and a half block's distance, I muttered to Mario, "Clueless! He's clueless. Time doesn't fly, it stands still. I'm going to be pregnant forever!"

Although I sincerely felt that way that night, I think the truth is actually somewhere in between. The days do, indeed, sometimes crawl, but the years race by.

What does this have to do with "dating" our children? *Webster's New World College Dictionary* defines a date as "an appointment for a set time, especially a social engagement (with a person of the opposite sex)." *Cambridge Advanced Learner's Dictionary* (Cambridge University Press, 2004) defines a date as "an engagement to go out socially with another person, often out of (romantic) interest" or " to regularly spend time with someone you wish to have a (romantic) relationship with."

Remove the references to romance and you have our goal: an appointment, set for a specific time, to go out socially with another person with whom you wish to have a relationship! It is a desire to get to know and to be known.

After careers, church, committees, and the general busyness of life, how much unplanned, unstructured, one-on-one time would we happen to have with our children? A recent study found it to be about 120 seconds a week! Two minutes of weekly intimate conversation are not likely to bring about much in the way of training a child's or teenager's heart. As in all the rest of life, if it's important, we schedule it in; we make time for it.

The year was 1983 and I was talking to a group of 7th and 8th grade girls. These were girls who came from great families; their fathers were elders and deacons in the church and leaders in their community. As part of a discussion leading up to the topic of discipleship and passing on their faith, I asked the question, "What is your favorite memory with your father?"

After a few minutes of silence followed by reminiscing, each of them told a story about a time spent with their fathers in a local father-daughter program sponsored by the neighborhood YMCA. Although a good program, it was for 1st and 2nd graders! The most recent meaningful experience these 13- and 14-year-old girls could remember having with their dads was at age eight. If we don't plan it, it won't just happen.

There are two types of dates: **listening dates** and **teaching dates**. Both are necessary in reaching the heart of our children. A listening date involves exactly what the name implies — you listening. When we lived in Dallas, two blocks away from our home was a convenience store that sold frozen slush drinks. Every Saturday morning, Mario made it a point to take Laura, our eldest, on a "slush date." Together they would stroll the two blocks to the store, buy a drink, and sit on the curb and talk. After a slow stroll home, he would get a kiss from Laura, drop his barely touched drink in the trash can and say, "Hey, Will, want to go get a slush?" Thus began the weekly slush parade.

There's something about walking side by side that brings out conversation in even the most shy and reclusive child. Instead of the rather forced stare across the table, it's a more natural flow-of-consciousness conversation. After the second week of this, the clerk at the store quit openly laughing every time Mario walked in, and the trash men gave up remarking on the number of slush cups in our garbage. With an investment of 30 minutes per child, Mario got a weekly glimpse inside the windows of their souls.

There are two types of dates: listening dates and teaching dates.

What about teaching dates? What do we teach? How do we decide what they need to hear? And how do we keep it from becoming a stern-faced lecture where we talk and they glaze over, uninterested, bored, and disengaged?

Few of us would tackle a new job or project without a plan or agenda. We want to approach scheduling "teaching moments" with our kids the same way. Consider three things when deciding what areas you need to address with your child.

One: What issues, hurts, pains, or concerns have you heard in your listening dates with them? If your child brings any of these things up, he or she has given you an opening, albeit tiny and tender, into this area of his or her heart and life. That's a great place to start.

Two: Watch your child. Watch her relationships with friends. Watch his attitudes during sports. Become the greatest student of, and expert concerning your child. There is a huge benefit in doing so.

Probably the most mis-taught Bible verse on parenting is Proverbs 22:6: *"Train up a child in the way he should go, and when he is old he will not depart from it."* An entire generation was taught that this verse meant that if we taught our children right from wrong, if we had them memorizing scripture, then when they were older they would not walk away from their faith. Have you known any kids from solid, evangelical homes who leave behind their faith when they leave for college? According to a recent study by Focus on the Family, 75 percent of all children from a Christian home walk away from their faith during college! Not all college kids, but 75 percent of those from Christian homes. It's a statistic that sends chills down the spine of parents. So, the question is, is Proverbs 22:6 wrong?

The problem lies in our interpretation of the verse. A more accurate understanding of it might be, "Train up a child toward his natural bent, because even when he is old, he will not depart from it." Our children are hard-wired to be a certain way. Do you have an artistic, creative child? Could he be forced to become an accountant? Possibly, but he would be miserable because that's not his natural bent. Do you have a child who loves numbers, order, and details? Could she be convinced to pursue a career in the arts? Probably, but she would be continually frustrated because that's not how she is hard-wired; it's not her natural bent. Is his natural bent to be hard-charging and competitive? Great! Teach him to be focused and goal-oriented toward things that have eternal significance. We need great Christian leaders. Is her natural bent to be introspective and cautious? Fabulous! Help her learn to use that gift, to think and be logical and bold. We desperately need great Christian thinkers. Train up a child toward his natural bent because even when he is old he will not depart from it. As we become experts on our children, we'll see those issues that need teaching and addressing.

Three: Watch your children's friends. If you see an issue or attitude that needs addressing in their friends' lives, it either does or will need addressing in your child's life. If Emily's friends have begun to go from encouraging and sweet to merciless gossips during car pool, now is the time to start teaching her what God has to say about the tongue and its use. It is significantly easier to build good character than to discipline out bad habits. Proactive is always better than reactive. What about Billy? As soon as you hear bad language from his friends, that's the time to go get ice cream sundaes and have a discussion about how a Godly man uses his words. Be proactive, rather than reactive.

Unfortunately, there's a part of us that loves to be like the proverbial ostrich and stick our heads in the sand. It's the "hear no evil, see no evil" mentality. We would rather look the other way when something is painful or ugly or wrong. I know it is true of me.

When we first got married, my husband used to say, "De Nile is more than a river in Egypt; it's my wife's middle name." When we are out for a walk in the park and come upon a couple engaged in inappropriate physical activity on a park bench, my tendency is to point the other way and say, "Wow! Look at those beautiful mallards! Who can tell me how we know they're male by their coloration?"

Unpleasant embarrassment averted, right? Wrong! My children saw that couple and assumed that, because I said nothing about it, their behavior must have been appropriate. Instead, here is a chance to sit down later and discuss with my kids what the Bible says about honoring one another and what a Godly relationship looks like before marriage.

Be proactive, not reactive! It is significantly easier and less costly to teach the foundations of this concept now, using someone else as an example, than the day before your son's or daughter's first date.

When a friend of ours gave birth to a severely handicapped child, she said, "Walk beside me on this journey and learn of pain and suffering second hand. It's a much less costly way to learn a lesson that everyone must eventually learn."

That's the heart of what we want to accomplish on our "dates" with our children. To unemotionally, away from the heat of the battle, teach them biblical truths that will mold their character and shape their hearts. If you are anything like me, you read that and think, "Great idea, but I'm already overwhelmed by all the things in my life. How do I add in one more? I already blink and my kids are a year older. I don't want to look back and have regrets at the things I wish I had taught them. But I'm too overwhelmed to get started on another to-do list."

I'm with you! As my husband is fond of saying, "You can't stuff two pounds of flour in a one-pound sack." So, how can we be deliberate about starting, but make it as fun and as effortless as possible?

When our children were young, we began having a yearly parenting summit. It might be anything from a weekend at a hotel to an afternoon at a friend's house. The only priorities are that it be quiet and distraction-free. We made manila folders with blank paper for each of the children. Starting with the oldest, we would pray for them individually, saying something like, "Lord, we only have ____ years left with this precious child before she leaves home. Would you please show us what she needs to learn in order to be ready to leave our home and thrive. As we discuss her, please give us wisdom to know how to best parent her."

Then we would begin to make two lists. One list was practical things that child still needed to learn how to do based on his age. It could be anything from tying shoes, to learning to make a bed, to learning to read, changing a tire, to balancing a checkbook, doing laundry, or applying for a job. The other list contained spiritual things they still needed to learn. This list contained anything from obeying cheerfully and **Be proactive, not reactive!** quickly, to returning kindness for evil, to persevering through difficult times, being diligent, being truthful, or learning to joyfully serve others, thereby serving Christ himself.

After prayerfully making the list, we would choose the top three things on each list. These became our goals for the year for that child. After praying for wisdom to find specific ways to teach these concepts, we would move on to the next child. The day ended with us scheduling a date for a six-month review to see whether we were actually intentionally, deliberately finding ways to work on those issues with our children.

One year, the top item on our list for our beautiful, blonde-haired, blue-eyed, precocious (read "into everything") three year old's list was to learn the blessing of obedience. For weeks, we practiced the family saying of, "Obedience brings...." He would respond with, "Blessings!" We would continue, "Disobedience brings...." To that, Daniel would respond, "Pain!"

One place this child's disobedience always showed up was at a mall. All admonitions to stay beside Mommy or hold Dad's hand disappeared when met with the plethora of delightful sights, sounds, and smells of the local mall. After getting a babysitter for all of the other children, we drove to the mall and practiced the disobedience/obedience rule at the entrance. With a quick "hold Daddy's hand," we entered.

Initially obedient, it took only a few moments before this sweet child was off and running, answering the sirens' call of the toy store window. Rather than grabbing his shirt or wrestling him back, Mario and I stepped behind a large potted tree about five feet away. After 60 seconds of delighting his senses at the toy store window, Daniel started to sense that something was wrong. After slowly looking to the left, then to the right, he realized he was lost and dissolved into a puddle of tears on the floor.

Twenty seconds later, a well-meaning grandmotherly woman approached Daniel. At that moment, we stepped from behind the ficus and said, "He's ours. We're learning a very hard lesson about obedience." She looked us up and down, assessing our fitness as parents, then said, "Good for you. Better for him!" With that, she walked off and we gathered a very recalcitrant, sorrowful child in our arms.

After a few moments of reassuring and comforting, we asked, "Daniel, did you obey us?"

Sadly, he answered, "No."

"Daniel, obedience brings...."

"Blessing."

"Disobedience brings...."

"Pain."

We knew that this was an issue this precious little one needed to learn. Was there a very real possibility that we might actually lose him in a crowded place someday? Absolutely! How much better it was to teach him the same lesson in a controlled, safe environment where he was never more than five feet away from us.

That's a proactive lesson — a date with a purpose. As my friend, Dave Jones, told me, "Treat your children as if you won't have them tomorrow. Train them as if they won't have you tomorrow."

Chapter Four

What Makes It Work?

One of the best things you can do to assure success in teaching difficult, abstract truths to your children is to learn to talk in stories. It's what Jesus did for us in the parables; He took abstract concepts and gave flesh to them. It's one thing for me to say to my children, "Sarcasm is mean, and as funny and witty as it may seem to you at the time, it hurts the other person."

On a really good day, they may hear it; on a regular day, I'm just a talking head. It's quite another when I say, "If I took this knife (which I obviously won't — this is just an example) and cut my flesh, would it hurt? Yes! Could I cover it up with a band aid and pretend it didn't hurt? Yes. But will it really take a while, maybe a long while to heal? And even after it heals, will there still be a scar?"

The word sarcasm literally means "to cut the flesh!" That's what sarcasm is; it cuts the flesh and causes pain that must heal. Words disappear, but word pictures remain in the minds of our kids. For a long time, every time that child sees a band-aid, he'll be reminded of the cost of sarcasm! That's much more effective than just saying, "Be nice."

There's one other essential element to effectively teach life-changing truths to our children. These truths must be grounded and supported by scripture. If I teach my children good, moral lessons, that's all they are — good and moral, not necessarily life-changing.

And they may very likely be simply my personal preference. When our children are babies, almost everything is a matter of our preference. We choose what they wear, what they eat, when they sleep, and where they go. As our children get older, we must move away from personal preference and toward scriptural principles. "I can't go to the movies with you guys. My mom and dad won't let me see PG-13 movies," works fine when the child is 10. The same approach does not prepare 15 year olds to wisely choose their own movies or 18 year old college freshmen to be discerning in their media choices.

Have you ever played the "whack-a-mole" game at an arcade or pizza parlor? Every time you successfully knock one mole back into his hole, two more pop up. If we teach our children moralism or our personal preferences, the "moles," or issues, will continue to pop up in a multitude of variances. I don't know about you, but this game wears me out. I don't want to deal with the same issue in 20 different ways. I would rather teach the scriptural principle that applies to 20 different situations and let it permeate their hearts and their lives! My preferences will no longer be the authority in their lives once they reach a certain age and leave my home. How much better it would be, then, to have taught them the authority and the applicability of God's Word in our lives.

Let's go back to the previous example. If the only reason my son hasn't gone to an R-rated movie has been because I didn't allow it, is he likely to go see R-rated movies once he leaves my home? Absolutely. Why would he not? The external set of controls is gone. But, what if he has learned to play "Catch the Lie" (see Date #4) in reference to all media sources? What if he has really fleshed out, in his own personal life, what Romans 12:1-2 means and how it looks to live out the principles of: *"Therefore, I urge you brothers, in view of God's mercy to offer your bodies as living sacrifices, holy and pleasing to God — this is your spiritual act of worship. Do not conform any longer to the pattern of this world, but be transformed by the renewing of your mind."*

If he has learned to discern with respect to the media and has learned that scripture has something to say about his choices, he'll be much more likely to avoid the trash out there that masquerades as entertainment. If I teach my children scriptural principles, backed up by specific Bible verses, they are being slowly equipped to move out into the world. They will be ready not just to survive, but to soar.

Do you see how much more prepared this young man is to deal with "the world" and all it will throw at him than the young man who never moves beyond, "My dad says so"? The first young man has been taught not to offend his parents. It may be effective until he leaves home. The second young man has made the decision and his faith his own. He has learned the biblical principle, has a specific verse to back it up, and knows how to live out his faith with authenticity and integrity. That, my friends, is a changed life. It is also the slow demise of the dreaded "whack-a-mole" game. This young man has been equipped to soar.

To be a child is to be in process.

Let me offer three cautions before we move onto the specifics of some life-changing dates with your children. First, expect progress to be slow. Have you ever attempted the science project of making crystals with your children? After the chemicals are added, the exact temperature is reached by boiling, the mixture and stick are put into the perfect container. Then you wait. And wait. And wait. Just as you begin to despair that you will never, ever see results, the crystals finally begin to form.

They are tiny little specks of crystal, but it gives you hope that you may eventually see full-blown, mature crystals. Don't expect or demand more than that from your child. To be a child is to be in process. It's supposed to be messy and take a long time. Proverbs 22:15 tells us that: *"Foolishness is bound up in the heart of a child."*

It's part of being a child. It takes time to move from simply changing behavior by the force of our personalities or the authority of our positions to changing hearts so that they actually desire changed behavior themselves. It is a total paradigm shift. Don't get frustrated when you don't see immediate results. Teaching to change hearts and lives is a substantially lengthier endeavor than changing behavior. Just as the farmer prepares the field, sows the seed, and then waits until the next season to harvest the crops, we must be patient as we wait to see these principles take root in our children's lives. Although it may seem as if you've taught the same lesson over and over until you've grown weary of it, trust that those little seeds are opening. Tiny crystals really are forming, and in the next season — whenever that may be — you will reap the crop of mature, life-changing faith in your child. Don't grow weary; the continued effort is worth it! Galatians 6:9 encourages us: *"Let us not grow weary in doing good, for at the proper time we will reap a harvest if we do not give up."*

A second caution: As we work diligently on our children's lives and character, it is easy to become convinced that the outcome is up to us. Have you ever heard the difference between dogs and cats? A dog looks at you and says, "You love me. You feed me. You groom me. You play with me. You must be God!" Your cat looks at you and says, "You love me. You feed me. You groom me. You play with me. I must be God!"

Way too often, we put ourselves in the cat's position as it relates to our kids. We must be God. We must charge them. We need to remind ourselves that foundationally, our kids are in God's hands. He is not the tool that we use to bring about good behavior in our kids. We are the tool that He uses to bring about righteousness in them. Do you hear the subtle, but huge, difference there? We can lead them to water, but can we make them drink? Absolutely not. Our job is to spread the banquet before them, that, as the Psalmist says, that they might *"taste and see that the Lord is good"* (Psalm 34:8).

God's job is this: *"Being confident of this, that He who began a good work in you will carry it on to completion until the day of Christ Jesus"* (Philippians 1:6). We spread the banquet table before them, but only God can cause them to desire to eat. Don't despair when you don't yet see any crystals beginning to form or any crops sprouting. Some crops yield a harvest that quickly sprouts, while others take significantly longer. But you and I, though we plant, water, and fertilize, cannot make them grow any faster. The God who created, redeemed, and sustains the very universe is at work in the hearts of our children and He is bringing them to completion in due season — in His time.

In the next chapter, we will look at one last caution. What can you and I do that might actually get in the way, or hinder, our kids' spiritual growth?

Chapter Five

Punishment or Discipline?

As parents, we have a fundamental issue to decide. Do we want to parent for quiet homes or for life change? I absolutely love it when my home is peaceful and quiet. Those rare moments when everyone is working quietly and no major crisis — physical, emotional, academic, social, or spiritual — is happening, are delightful. But those moments are fleeting, and before long, someone will spill a glass of milk on the carpet (forbidden territory for all food and drinks), tattle on a sister, "accidentally" trip a brother, or roll their eyes at someone. I'm now back to that fundamental decision. Quiet or life change? Put differently, punishment or discipline?

Although we tend to use the words interchangeably, punishment and discipline are entirely different. *Punishment* stops a behavior. It achieves quiet. *Discipline* teaches a lesson and helps to change a heart.

Proverbs: 12 says: *"For whom the Lord loves, he corrects, even as a father the son in whom he delights."* The implication here is that not to discipline means not to love. The whole point of discipline is to get their attention, so that we can teach them a lesson. Discipline is never an end in itself. If the point is to get their attention, we'd better have something to say once we get it!

That brings us to the issue of our agenda or personal preference versus scriptural principles. Our kids will be significantly better off if we always take them to scripture for the "why" of discipline. Our goal here is that they would begin to view God's Word as the ultimate authority in their lives rather than my word. It's a practical issue. God's Word is perfect. My words are not. It will always be here; I will not.

Let's look at an example of the difference between punishment and discipline. Sophie, 3, and Adam, 4, are arguing over whose turn it is with the ball. Punishment says, "Give me that ball. It's going in time out until you two can share it nicely." The behavior was stopped. Peace and quiet were returned. But did either child learn anything? They learned to be quieter when they argue.

Discipline says, "Children, bring me the ball. Sophie, go sit on my bed and wait for me. Adam, go sit on your bed and wait for me. I'll be in to talk to each of you."

Yes, we've stopped the behavior, but we're now going to take it further. The first thing we did was separate them so that each heart, each issue, each child can be dealt with privately.

Have you ever had someone approach you publicly with something you did wrong? I am so embarrassed by the fact that others are listening that it's very difficult for me to hear the correction or the principle. I would be able to learn the lesson much better if it were taught privately. I want to offer my children the same courtesy and opportunity, so they are sent to separate locations.

Why both kids? It takes two to argue, so two most likely need a heart lesson. It's why we should never ask, "Who started this argument?" It doesn't matter because both chose to engage in the argument. We also never ask, "Why did you do that?" The answer is sin. You know your kids, and you can probably guess who started it. But one wrong assumption and one child is gloating because he got away with it and the other is grieving because they were falsely accused. Neither one learned anything. They don't really want justice; they want parity. They want to make sure that both of them were "dealt with," so they're sent opposite directions in order to deal with different issues.

You now go to Sophie in your room and have the following conversation: "Sophie, I know that's your new ball that you just got for your birthday and that Adam took it away from you. That was wrong on his part and he will apologize to you later for that. But, you should not have yelled at him. You returned evil for evil, but God wants you to learn to return kindness for evil. Remember the story of how King Saul was chasing David and trying to kill him? David and his men went into a cave and found Saul sleeping there. Instead of getting even with Saul, or returning evil for evil, David left him there and returned kindness for evil. That's what God wants for us, Sophie. He wants us to trust Him in those hard times and to return kindness to the other person. Can you go out there in a few minutes and return kindness to Adam, even though he gave you evil?"

There is a lot to be learned about our hearts and Godly behavior from being wronged.

At this point, hopefully Sophie replies, "Yes, Mom."

"Good choice, sweetie. Let's pray together and ask God to help you return kindness for evil when it's hard."

Do you see how much more happens in Sophie's heart than having heard, "Quit crying, Sophie. Here's your ball back. Adam, go to your room." If Sophie were any older, it would be the perfect time to read Romans 12:17 & 19 together: *"Do not repay anyone evil for evil. Do not take revenge, my friends, but leave room for God's wrath, for it is written, 'It is mine to avenge; I will repay,' says the Lord."* Then we would discuss what revenge is and why it dishonors and displeases God.

There's a lot to be learned about our hearts and Godly behavior from being wronged. If she learns this lesson early, Sophie has the privilege of being prepared later to deal with friends who gossip, teammates who grab all the glory, or fellow employees who steal the credit for her ideas. She will have learned to trust a sovereign God to defend her. How much better to teach the principle that applies to 20 different situations and let it permeate her heart, her actions, and her life.

We now go to Adam to have a conversation somewhat similar to the following. "Adam, I know you were frustrated because

Sophie wouldn't share her new ball with you. But it was wrong for you to take it away from her. If Jesus were here, Adam, would you let him have a long turn with the ball?"

Adam: "Yes, Mom. But Sophie's not Jesus!"

"Let's read a story together from your Bible, Adam. In Matthew 25, Jesus is separating the sheep (those are the people who know and love Him) from the goats (those are the people who don't know Him)."

I'll read Matthew 25:34-40, which says, *"Then the king will say to those on the right, 'Come, you who are blessed by my father; take your inheritance, the kingdom prepared for you since the creation of the world. For I was hungry and you gave me something to eat, I was thirsty and you gave me something to drink, I was a stranger and you invited me in, I needed clothes and you clothed me, I was in prison and you came to visit me.' Then the righteous will answer him, 'Lord, when did we see you hungry and feed you, or thirsty and give you something to drink? When did we see you a stranger and invite you in, or needing clothes and clothe you? When did we see you sick or in prison and go to visit you?' The King will reply, 'I tell you the truth, whatever you did for one of the least of these brothers of mine, you did for me.'"*

"Do you hear what Jesus is saying, Adam? You may never get the chance to actually share that ball with Jesus, but when you share it with the least of these, with Sophie, it's like you shared it with Jesus himself. Would you share the ball with Jesus if he were here? Then share with Sophie and it's actually credited to you as having shared with Jesus.

We must always discipline our kids with huge amounts of grace.

"That's the principle I want you to begin to learn, Adam. But now we need to talk about something else. When you took the ball from Sophie, you took honor from her. I would like you to go back out there and restore honor to her. First, you need to apologize and ask her forgiveness in order to help restore the relationship. Since the argument was over a toy, I think it would be nice if you offered to play whatever she wants for the next 15 minutes. Let's pray together and ask God to help you treat Sophie the way you would treat Jesus. Can you do that, son?"

Hopefully Adam responds, "Yes, ma'am."

Do you see how much more Adam has learned than "It's not nice to take a ball away from someone"? He's learned that the way he treats other people matters intimately to God, and he's learned how to restore a fractured relationship. Yes, it's more work, but it's infinitely more valuable than, "Stop arguing. Give me the ball until you two can share."

It's discipline-disciple making. It's seizing the moment both to stop a behavior and to teach a heart lesson that will help to shape Christ-like character in a young life.

Someone is invariably asking right about now, "But if I always use scripture to discipline my kids, won't they grow to resent the Bible?" The answer to that is a resounding yes, unless we do two things.

First, we must always discipline our kids with huge amounts of grace. If we are angry, they won't hear the lesson; they will only hear a raised voice, anger, and condemnation. On many occasions, I have said to my kids, "I am really angry right now. Go to your rooms. Give me five minutes before the Throne of Grace to calm myself down and then we will deal with this issue."

In my weakness, my kids have now learned:

1) Don't speak when you're angry. You'll regret what you say;

2) The way to deal with anger, or any issue, is to take it to the Throne of Grace and let God help you deal with it; and,

3) Even my parents aren't perfect, but they get their strength from God.

The old adage "More is caught than taught" is true. Our children are watching everything we do to see if it matches with what we say. Never discipline in anger. Always discipline with grace.

Secondly, our kids will resent us using scripture as a tool in their lives unless they see us turning it on our own lives with the same (or greater) zeal that we turn it on their lives. Do they see us consistently in the Word? A casual relationship with scripture guarantees a casual relationship with God.

Our children are not mind-readers. Unless I tell them what God is teaching me and where He is molding, shaping, breaking, and disciplining me, they will assume I simply have it all together (or not) because I'm a grown-up. If they see scripture as alive and real in my life, it will be much easier for them to want it as alive and real in their own lives.

That takes us back to spreading out the banquet table before our kids so that they can taste and see that He is good. They can see Him as real and active and alive in their lives. Remember, be proactive. The "dates" are organized by teaching topic or subject. You can pick the one area in your child's life where they most need to see the truths of scripture worked out in their lives. Feel free to take a word picture or example and use it in an entirely different way if that fits what your child needs to learn. Change the setting if that makes sense for your family. Be creative. The key is to pick a time and place, and set a "date" with them.

Take one of these examples and ask God to show you how to use it in your child's life. It's not about technique; it's about life-changing experiences with your son or daughter as they encounter the Living God. These dates can be life-changing, disciple-making, relationship-building time together as we have the incredible privilege of watching the Word of God become alive and real in their lives.

McPrayers

"DO NOT BE ANXIOUS ABOUT ANYTHING, BUT IN EVERY-
THING, BY PRAYER AND SUPPLICATION, WITH THANKS-
GIVING, PRESENT YOUR REQUESTS TO GOD."
PHILIPPIANS 4:6

A good, deep, rich prayer life is absolutely essential to a growing Christian. Few of us would argue the fact that if we had few, or sporadic, conversations with our spouse, the relationship would suffer deeply. Yet in this day of multi-tasking and hurried lifestyles, it's too easy to relegate our prayer time to a quick "check-in" in the morning, a cursory blessing at meals, and a "Lord, help me here," as we race through the day.

We want our kids to see the need for developing real, not snatched, prayer lives. How do we show them the cost of casual prayer and the rewards of real prayer? By taking them with us to the Throne of Grace!

If your family is anything like ours, way too often you find yourself in the "drive through" lane of your local fast food restaurant on the way home from a busy day. Here is a perfect teachable moment! As the two of you are eating, you can have the following conversation:

"Abby, this 'to go' food tastes pretty good right now, because we were both really hungry. What if 'to go' meals were all we ever ate? Although they taste pretty good and meet an immediate, urgent need, we would eventually be unhealthy because of them. We couldn't live for long like this, could we? We need full course meals on a regular basis to remain healthy."

I think we tend to try that same thing with our prayer lives. We try to live on quickly grabbed 'to go' prayers as we hurry through our days. Just like our bodies would starve, our souls will too. I don't want to starve either one, do you? A healthy meal usually involves four things: vegetables, fruit, grains, and protein. A healthy prayer life involves four things also. It includes:

Adoration — praising and acknowledging God as who He is,

Confession — admitting our sins and asking for His forgiveness,

Thanksgiving — thanking God for who He is and what He's done, and

Supplication — asking God to will and to work in the world.

Look, it spells out ACTS, so it's easy to remember. Can you and I agree to pray together for the next seven days so that we start to learn to feed our souls and our relationships with the Lord the same healthy way we want to feed our bodies? Would you rather set aside 15 minutes before school or after dinner? Let's hold each other accountable to not try to live on 'to go' prayers."

Date #2

Prayer Walk

"IS ANY ONE OF YOU IN TROUBLE? HE SHOULD PRAY. IS
ANY ONE OF YOU SICK? HE SHOULD CALL THE ELDERS OF
THE CHURCH TO PRAY OVER HIM AND ANOINT HIM
WITH OIL IN THE NAME OF THE LORD. AND THE PRAYER
OFFERED IN FAITH WILL MAKE THE SICK PERSON WELL;
THE LORD WILL RAISE HIM UP."
JAMES 5:13-15a

All around us, people are suffering. Marriages are stressed, careers fizzle, children are sick, students struggle, neighbors argue. Our natural tendency is to want to step in and help fix things, to try to right the ills of the world ourselves. Have you ever heard anyone say, "I can't do anything else, but I'll pray." We relegate prayer to the bottom of the list as far as what we can do in the world.

We have it backwards; prayer is meant to be the primary work of the believer! In our lives and our associations with others, we model either Ishmael or Isaac to our children. Are we Ishmael — do we act first, then ask God to come behind us and bless our actions? Or are we Isaac? Do we ask God to work and then wait on Him to lead?

The greatest work to be done in our neighborhoods and our hearts is the work of prayer. If we involve ourselves and our kids, it teaches our kids:

1) to be concerned for the needs of those around them,

2) that the greatest solution to those needs will be found, not in our ability to "fix it," but in God.

"Mike, I'm really concerned about some of our neighbors. Some of them are dealing with really hard things. I know we're supposed to pray for them, but I tend to get so busy that I forget to. I have an idea. Want to do this with me? Let's meet tomorrow at 7:00 and we'll walk up one side of our block and down the other side. As we pass each house, we'll pray for the family inside — for their marriage, jobs, and school. We can pray that if they know God, He'll give them a deep, rich relationship with Him and help them to live what they believe. If they don't know God, we'll pray that they would hear the truth and come to a saving knowledge of Christ.

Do we ask God to work and then wait on Him to lead?

"If we do this every Tuesday, eventually some of our neighbors may notice and ask what we're doing. As we explain it to them, we can tell them that we would love to know any specific prayer requests they might have since we pray for them and all the rest of our neighbors every Tuesday morning.

"We can end up back in our front yard and finish our prayer walk with prayer for our family and for our nation's leaders. What an exciting way to get involved in our neighbor's lives in a way that will count for all of eternity! What do you think? Should we start tomorrow?"

Date #3

Media & Cultural Influences

"FINALLY, BROTHERS, WHATEVER IS TRUE, WHATEVER IS HONORABLE, WHATEVER IS JUST, WHATEVER IS PURE, WHATEVER IS LOVELY, WHATEVER IS COMMENDABLE, IF THERE IS ANY EXCELLENCE, IF THERE IS ANYTHING WORTHY OF PRAISE, THINK ABOUT THESE THINGS."
PHILIPPIANS 4:8

Would any of us want Hollywood to disciple or shape our children's minds? The answer is probably a resounding, "NO." Yet at an alarming rate, popular culture does affect our children. Consider these statistics from Probe Ministries:

The average high school graduate, from birth until graduation, has spent 11,000 hours in formal classroom education.

The same graduate has spent 22,000 hours watching TV!

Those 22,000 hours included:
16,000 homicides

200,000 acts of violence
640,000 commercials

This same student also watches an additional six movies, videos, or DVDs a week.

As horrifying as these statistics seem, why should this concern us? Aren't all of these television shows and movies just telling stories? All entertainment is making a statement. It's a question of what worldview, what belief system about all of life, are they espousing? Of those involved in the television industry, 93 percent are secularists, rarely attending any religious services of any kind.

Again, statistics from Probe Ministries show the leading sources of social influence on our children, in order of influence, are:

Movies
TV
Internet
Books
Music
Public policy
Law
Family

Do you notice a glaring omission? Although we're glad that "family" made the list, "church" is no longer even listed in the top 12 sources of influence. The danger should be obvious to us. We are, indeed, in a battle for the hearts and minds of our children.

"Hey kids, I have a gift here for someone. It's a piece of chocolate. And it's not just any chocolate; it's Hershey's milk chocolate with almonds and toffee! Who would like this piece of candy? Ok, Sarah Grace, since you raised your hand first, it's yours. Enjoy it!

"I have another gift in this pretty box. Daddy grew up in Holland, and until I met him I had never heard of Dutch chocolates. Every time Oma and Opa came to see us they would bring us some of those wonderful chocolates. Dutch chocolate has a higher cocoa content than what we're used to, so the taste almost explodes in your mouth. And it has a much higher butter fat content, so it almost melts in your mouth. It is absolutely amazing!

"In this box, I have Dutch chocolates. But they're not just any Dutch chocolates. They are fat-free, sugar-free Dutch chocolates. That means you can eat them all day long without any stomachaches and without gaining an ounce in weight. Would you like to trade me that plain little piece of chocolate for this fabulous one? I thought you might be willing to trade; most people would.

Unless we know the truth, it will be easy to believe a lie.

"But there is a problem. Go ahead and open the pretty box. What is in it?

"Nothing! It's empty. Fat-free, sugar-free Dutch chocolates don't really exist. It's a lie. But I can get you to devalue and even give up the very real, very good chocolate you held in your hand if I can get you to believe in the lie.

"Kids, that's what the world around us does to us if we're not careful. Unless we know the truth, it will be easy to believe a lie. We don't want our culture to tell us what to value, to pursue or to look like, do we? If we let the world decide the focus of our hearts and minds, it will turn out to be as empty and as unfulfilling as this box.

"Instead, let's agree to help each other focus on 'whatever.' We'll start by memorizing Philippians 4:8 together and then we'll ask God to help us look at everything in our lives through the filter of whether or not it fits the 'whatever' challenge in this verse. And as soon as we have all helped each other learn it, I have some real Dutch chocolates for us to enjoy together. Let's get started!"

Date #4

Catch the Lie

"BUT IF ANYONE CAUSES ONE OF THESE LITTLE ONES
WHO BELIEVE IN ME TO SIN, IT WOULD BE BETTER FOR
HIM TO HAVE A LARGE MILLSTONE HUNG AROUND HIS
NECK AND TO BE DROWNED IN THE DEPTHS OF THE SEA."
MATTHEW 18:6

No movie or television show ever simply just tells a story; it is also making a statement, espousing a worldview. Behind some very entertaining movies are some very subtle lies. When we turn on the movie, we let the worldview, complete with lies, into our minds and our homes. Our goal needs to be to teach our children to watch with a discerning attitude. If our children never learn to watch and recognize the lies, we leave them at a distinct disadvantage when they leave home. They will most likely watch TV and movies at some point in their lives; let's teach them to "learn to discern."

"We're going to start a new tradition in our family today, kids. We're going to learn to play a game called, 'Catch the Lie.' In almost every movie, no matter how good it is, there are some things that disagree with scripture, things that go against God's Word. We want to learn to recognize those things so that they don't affect our minds and how we think. When we hear something over and over, first we get used to it, then we grow comfortable with it, and then finally we accept it as truth whether we meant to or not. That's why we want to learn to look for and recognize the lies.

"So while we watch the movie tonight, I want everyone to see how many lies they can find. In the car on the way home, we'll see how many everyone found and talk about them. You ready? Let's see who can find the most."

If we are comfortable with lies, then we'll accept them as truth.

We expect lots of "lies" in movies that are rated PG (parental guidance recommended) or PG-13 (parental guidance for anyone under 13), but we like to think that a G (general audience) rated movie would be fairly innocuous and safe. Here is a partial list of "lies" my children caught in a G-rated movie involving a girl of regular status who finds herself suddenly elevated to a very high social status:

She lies.

She is disrespectful to her mother.

She thinks having a boyfriend and getting kissed will make her happy.

The clothes that some of the girls wear are very immodest.

She takes revenge on a group of cheerleaders, smashing an ice cream cone on one of their shirts while the audience cheers her on.

Even though the movie is cute and everyone learns their lesson in the end, you can see how subtle lies creep in. If we address them, our kids will recognize them the next time they see them and know the truth.

Date #5

Modesty

I ALSO WANT WOMEN TO DRESS MODESTLY, WITH
DECENCY AND PROPRIETY, NOT WITH BRAIDED HAIR OR
GOLD OR PEARLS, OR EXPENSIVE CLOTHES, BUT WITH
GOOD DEEDS, APPROPRIATE FOR WOMEN WHO PROFESS
TO WORSHIP GOD."
1 TIMOTHY 2:9

Have you gone to the mall lately and looked at the way
some teenagers dress? Did it discourage and dishearten you? More
importantly, does it discourage and dishearten you that you're
fighting this battle in your own home?

Kids, as a rule, want to look like other kids. Most kids go
through a stage where they want to feel like "part" of the group
before they grow bold enough to rise above the group. Our goal is
to give them a reason to rise above the norm. There is very little in
our culture to encourage our daughters to dress modestly. We must
give them the encouragement and the reason to do so.

Our goal is to be proactive whenever possible. That means
that the topic of modesty is best addressed before it becomes a real
issue. Look at you daughter's peer group. If this has become an
issue with anyone, it is time to address it in your own home. This
date is most effective between a father and daughter. But if dad is

not there physically, spiritually, or emotionally, mom must take the initiative. This one is too important to let go.

"Mandy, let's go for an ice-cream date tonight. I have something I would like for us to look at.

"Mandy, this is one of the teen magazines that are so popular today. I want us to look at a couple of things about this magazine."

Spend a few minutes briefly looking through the magazine. The goal is to point out how inappropriately the models dress. You will have no trouble finding examples of immodesty!

"Mandy, what is modesty?

"That's close. It means 'not forward, behaving according to a standard of what's proper, decent, and pure.' The question, Mandy, is who gets to decide what that standard is? If we let the world, or culture, decide our standards, they will always be changing according to the whims of the times. I don't consider that much of a standard, do you? If you were going to buy a pound of really good chocolates for $10, and I took your money and handed you about a half of a pound, you would feel cheated wouldn't you? What would you think if I said that according to my standards of measurement, that was a pound? You would want us to be using the same standard, wouldn't you? That is called an 'absolute standard.' It doesn't change according to someone's opinion.

Standards don't change according to someone's — or society's — opinion.

"The greatest absolute standard is God's Word. It doesn't change from person to person or from age to age. So let's look at this magazine from God's perspective of what is 'proper, decent and pure.' Do you think these outfits would qualify? You're right, they wouldn't. A girl who dresses like this is trying to draw attention to herself, showing off her body, trying to feel important because of what she looks like and how she can get people to notice her. That's not beauty, that's manipulation!

"Let's look at what the Bible says we're to do. Philippians 2:3-4 says, '*Do nothing from rivalry or conceit, but in humility count others more significant than yourselves. Let each of you look not only to his own interests, but also to the interests of others.*' Dressing like these models can in no way be considered as counting others as more significant than yourself. It causes men to think wrong thoughts and it causes competition and jealousy among women. There's a reason God doesn't want us to dress like this. It doesn't build each other up, it tears down. I would be pretty selfish if I did something that I knew ahead of time would make you fall down, or stumble wouldn't I? Some people call this type of clothes 'stumblewear.'

"It's possible to wear cute clothes without causing other people to stumble. Let's make it our goal as we buy your clothes from now on to make sure that we're not buying 'stumblewear.' I am so proud of you, sweetie, for wanting to dress in a way that honors the 'absolute standard' of decent and pure, and that pleases the Lord!"

For those of us with older daughters, there are two other discussions you might want to have over this "magazine" date.

1) These magazines are intentionally colorful, bright, shiny, and attractive to young girls. They are not just innocuous fashion magazines that deal with common teenage issues. They have a worldview at which most parents will be horrified. Take a few minutes and read through the titles of the articles and discuss why what they focus on should be horrifying to a Christian. If they know what is wrong with these magazines, they won't be tempted to "just take a look" when they see it at someone else's house. They'll say, "I know that's a lie, my dad and I looked at one together!"

2) You might want to take this opportunity to discuss with her what it means that men are attracted by visual stimuli and how that should affect the way she dresses and conducts herself around men.

Bounce

"THE EYE IS THE LAMP OF THE BODY. IF YOUR EYES ARE
GOOD, YOUR WHOLE BODY WILL BE FULL OF LIGHT. BUT IF
YOUR EYES ARE BAD, YOUR WHOLE BODY WILL BE FULL
OF DARKNESS. IF THEN THE LIGHT WITHIN YOU IS DARK-
NESS, HOW GREAT IS THAT DARKNESS!"
MATTHEW 6:22-23

Just as the mall and clothing provide a teaching opportunity
for our daughters, the same is true for our sons. Ours is a visually
provocative culture that throws constant sensual images at our
young men. From billboards to storefronts to commercials, the
bombardment is continual. How is a young man of integrity to deal
with it?

We had gone to the mall to look at Christmas decorations
and do a little shopping. I was walking along,
enjoying myself and visiting with my teenage
son, when all of the sudden his head turned 90
degrees to the left. He was now walking beside
me, but looking at his right shoulder. Thinking
this was some new bizarre teenage phenomenon, I said, "OK, I give
up. What on earth are you doing?"

**Train your boys
to "bounce."**

"I'm bouncing, Mom. Just bounce!" he answered.

We walked on in silence for a few moments before I replied, "Excuse me? I'm lost here."

"James 4:7," he insisted.

Just then my husband and older son walked up beside us. As they glanced to our right, I heard my husband whisper, "Bounce, boys, bounce!"

James 4:7 says, *"Submit to God, resist the devil, and he will flee from you."*

Unbeknownst to me, my husband had been using the mall as a teaching time with our sons. Since men are visual, he had taught them that at the first sign of visual temptation, they should choose to physically fight it, turning their whole body away from the sight. Hence, the "bounce."

To this day, when we pass an immodest billboard, sign, or woman, I'll hear them whisper, "Bounce, brother, bounce!"

Let's hear it for men of integrity, who "bounce."

Let's teach it to our sons!

Date #7

Sponges

"DO YOU NOT KNOW THAT FRIENDSHIP WITH THE
WORLD IS ENMITY WITH GOD?"
JAMES 4:4B

Are our children affected by their environment? Have you ever watched a television show or read a book with your children and later heard them acting it out? Does the same child who insists that he or she cannot memorize a poem for Language Arts class then repeats whole scenes of movie lines from their favorite movies?

Our kids think that they are impervious to being affected by the culture around them. Any parent who has heard them flaw-lessly parrot back those movie lines knows the truth. As in "Catch the Lie," half the battle is being aware that there is a battle. We're much more careful when we realize there's something at stake.

"Daniel, what do I have here? You're right, it's a sponge. What do you and a sponge have in common? Watch and I'll show you. If I put this dry sponge in a bowl full of clear water and then squeeze the sponge out over the sink, what comes out of the sponge? Right, clear water. Now, if I put a dry sponge in this bowl

The environment does affect our children.

47

full of red punch and then squeeze it out over the sink, what comes out of the sponge? Right, red liquid. The sponge naturally soaks up whatever is around and gives off that same thing. It would be pretty silly for us to expect a sponge soaked in red water to give off clear water when it was squeezed, wouldn't it?

"What does that say about what you and I need to surround ourselves with? I Corinthians 15:33 says, 'Do not be deceived; bad company ruins good morals.'

"We need to be careful about what we watch, what we read, and where we spend our time. It matters!"

Date #8

The Bible as a Treasure Map

"THE GRASS WITHERS, THE FLOWER FADES, BUT THE
WORD OF OUR GOD WILL STAND FOREVER."
ISAIAH 40:8

Have you ever felt like having a quiet time was just another thing to be crossed off your list? Like you did it just to have it done? Mechanically, woodenly, out of duty instead of out of hunger and delight? We want more than that for our kids.

We want our kids to want to go to the Word on a regular basis. Once they get to the Word, it is the Holy Spirit who writes it upon their heart. How can we give our kids a hint of all of the riches that wait for them there? How can we encourage them to go on a hunt for treasure just waiting for them?

Let's go on a treasure hunt together! Let's show them a purpose, a reason for diligent study of the Word.

"Sarah Grace, would you like to go on a treasure hunt? I have hidden a treasure somewhere in the house. It is something that you will absolutely love when you find it. Are you interested? Good! This will be fun. Are you ready? You may begin hunting."

Let your child hunt for as long as it takes until he or she begins to get frustrated at not being able to find it. Give her absolutely no clues at all. When she announces that she can't find the treasure unless you give some hints, pull out a treasure map.

"It's pretty impossible to find a treasure without an accurate map, isn't it? The treasure is out there, but we might search forever and never find it. We might give up and decide that it doesn't really exist. Or we might find something else, something way less than the treasure, and decide that this must be it. That it will do. But it's not the great treasure at all.

We want our kids to want to go to the Word on a regular basis.

"Is it the fault of the treasure that we cannot find it? No. We need something, don't we? We need a treasure map! Look what I have in my pocket — a treasure map."

Pull out a map of a specific room of your house, showing the placement of all furniture and an "X" marking the spot where the treasure is hidden.

"Let's study it together for a few minutes. Do you think you can find the treasure now? Go on and look for it.

"Good job, Sarah Grace! You found the treasure.

"You looked for a long time the first time around without ever finding it. This time you went right to it. What made the difference? You're right — a map! It's hard to find treasure without a treasure map.

"Did you know that God has all sorts of treasure waiting for you? He has great things to offer you for your whole life. He has also sent you a treasure map to help you find it.

"Do you want to see the map? It's right here in my hands — the Bible! It was fun to go on a treasure hunt with a map, wasn't it? But first, we studied the map together.

"If you'll study this map, it will show you all of that treasure God has waiting for you. Let's agree to go on a treasure hunt together every day for the next two weeks.

"We'll study God's map together and see what He has for us. Are you game?"

Date #9

The Bible as a Roadmap

"YOUR WORD IS A LAMP TO MY FEET AND A LIGHT TO MY
PATH."
PSALM 119:105

There are lots of systems, methods and people out there who purport to know the "truth" and to show our kids how to have "successful" lives. We want them to learn to go the source — the author, creator, sustainer — to find their way. Anything less causes wasted time, energy, and lives. Let's show them the futility of trying to figure it out on their own and the reason for going to the author.

"Mary Claire, I have a question for you. You're about to get your driver's license in a few weeks. I have a friend who just moved to Murieta, California. If I handed you the keys to my car in two weeks and told you to meet me at her house, could you get there?

"You don't think so? I think you actually would get there eventually, but let's list what might happen on the trip in the meantime."

Let them list everything they can think of that might happen on a trip with very little idea of where they are going.

"You would probably take a lot longer to get there than you really needed, wouldn't you? Do you think you would take several wrong roads? There would be lots of wasted time. How much gas might you use? A whole lot more than you needed to use. It would cost you a lot more than it needed to, wouldn't it? How about energy? Would you arrive there pretty worn out from a long, useless, costly trip?

"I really do think you would get there eventually on your own, but what if I handed you this before you left home? An Atlas — it's a map of every road between here and there.

Wouldn't a map make the journey easier?

"If we plotted your course, you would get there in significantly less time. You would spend less time getting lost, taking wrong turns and detours, and having to backtrack to get back to the right roads. You would use less money, resources, and energy. There would have been less distractions, diversions, and needless waste.

"It would be a way better way to make the journey, don't you think? It would seem pretty naive to set out on a trip of that magnitude without consulting a map first, wouldn't it?

"A lifetime is a lot more important than just a trip. God agrees. In fact he agrees so mush that He gave you a roadmap for all of life.

"I have that roadmap for life here in my hands. It's the Bible. Let's agree that you and I will not set out on even one day of this fabulous journey without first going to the roadmap! Would you like to have our quiet times together every morning this week before we set out? Let's meet at 7:00 tomorrow and get started."

Date #10

Life Is a Puzzle

"FOREVER, O LORD, YOUR WORD IS FIRMLY FIXED IN THE HEAVENS. YOUR FAITHFULNESS ENDURES TO ALL GENER-ATIONS; YOU HAVE ESTABLISHED THE EARTH AND IT STANDS FAST. IF YOUR LAW HAD NOT BEEN BY DELIGHT, I WOULD HAVE PERISHED IN MY AFFLICTION. I WILL NEVER FORGET YOUR PRECEPTS, FOR BY THEM YOU HAVE GIVEN ME LIFE."
PSALM 119:89-90, 92-93

It's not the same world you and I grew up in, is it? We desperately long to give our children the wonderful, peaceful world of Ozzie and Harriet on the old TV show *Leave it to Beaver*. Instead, the world is giving them genocide, world hunger, corruption at every turn, and a pervasive relativism that says, "As long as you're seeking, you'll find. Any truth is truth and they're all just as good. But in the meantime, you'd better serve yourself, because no one else will."

I don't know about you, but when I go to the grocery store to buy a pound of meat, I want the store and me to be using the same standard. I want us to mean the same thing when we say "pound." Otherwise, one of us is not going to be pleased with the transaction.

Very few people would argue with that logic. There must, then, be some objective standard! We want our kids to look at His Word as that absolute, objective standard. His Word is Truth. He is without shadow or change. We certainly can't say that about the world!

"Joel, I have a puzzle in this box. If I gave it to you, do you think you could work it? It's an absolutely beautiful picture. I bet you could!"

Hand your child the box and let him begin and work for a few minutes.

"Did I mention that there are about 20 pieces missing from this puzzle? Sorry about that. It will make it a little harder to succeed in making the picture, won't it? Keep trying, though."

After another minute or so.

"One other thing I forgot to mention, dear. That picture on the top of the box? It's not the real one for the puzzle. I lost the top awhile ago and put a different one on the box. So the picture you're looking at for an example, or guidance, is not even the real picture.

"Missing pieces and a wrong box-top picture make it impossible to finish this puzzle and do it well, doesn't it son? We don't even know what it should look like, do we? We really do need all of the pieces and the top of the box, a correct picture of the real thing, to be able to succeed. Losing these two things has set us up to fail.

"That's what our culture has done to us in life, son. There are pieces missing. Things that God means for us to pursue and to value that our culture says we don't need at all anymore. We have no picture left to use as a model. Our culture doesn't give us a picture of what a Godly young man or woman, a Godly son or daughter, or a young man of integrity looks like.

"Even more so than working a puzzle, we desperately need all of the pieces and the picture here, but God has given us all of the pieces and the picture of what it is supposed to look like. It's right here in His Word.

"Let's not set ourselves up to fail like we did with this puzzle. Let's find all of the pieces and see what a young man of integrity looks like, according to the absolute standard. Let's start tonight!"

Ready, Aim, Fire!

"ALL SCRIPTURE IS BREATHED OUT BY GOD AND PROF-
ITABLE FOR TEACHING, FOR REPROOF, FOR CORRECTION,
AND FOR TRAINING IN RIGHTEOUSNESS, THAT THE MAN
OF GOD MAY BE COMPETENT, EQUIPPED FOR EVERY GOOD
WORK."
II TIMOTHY 3:16

There is an old adage that goes something like this, "If you aim at nothing, you'll probably hit it every time." What are our kids aiming for? What is the target?

Psalm 127 speaks of our children as arrows. What is the purpose of an arrow? To hit a target! Hard-wired into all of us is the desire to do something that matters, that lasts, that counts. No one likes to do things that count for nothing and that are an absolute waste of time and energy. Busy work frustrates even a young child.

Proverbs 29:18 tells us, *"Where there is no vision, the people perish."* Let's give our kids a vision. Let's help aim our arrows at the only target that matters.

"Laura, I have a challenge for you. You are a very good athlete. If I hand you this bow and arrow, do you think you could hit the bulls-eye? Maybe? Here you go, let's try. Show me how close you can get to hitting the center of the target."

The issue here is that you have given your child the bow and arrow, but there is no target in sight.

"Why can't you hit the target? Because there is not a target in sight. Can we hit a target we don't have in our sights? Probably not. We have to know what we're aiming for, don't we? We have to know our goal, our purpose.

What are our kids aiming for?

"The world around us moves the target all of the time or even tells us that there is no real target. It's up to you to just aim wherever you think is right. That doesn't leave us much chance of really hitting the target, does it? I don't want to shoot wild, ineffective, wasted arrows that never get near the bulls-eye, do you? That's pretty frustrating.

"But God gave us an exact target for which to aim! It's right here in the Bible.

"Let's figure out where the target is, what our goal is, together. Let's aim at a real target that lasts and matters. Let's know what we're aiming for."

Date #12

Training to Win the Race

"DO YOU NOT KNOW THAT IN A RACE ALL THE RUNNERS COMPETE, BUT ONLY ONE RECEIVES THE PRIZE? SO RUN THAT YOU MAY OBTAIN IT. EVERY ATHLETE EXERCISES SELF-CONTROL IN ALL THINGS. THEY DO IT TO RECEIVE A PERISHABLE WREATH, BE WE ARE IMPERISHABLE. SO I DO NOT RUN AIMLESSLY; I DO NOT BOX AS ONE BEATING THE AIR. BUT I DISCIPLINE MY BODY AND KEEP IT UNDER CONTROL, LEST AFTER PREACHING TO OTHERS I MYSELF SHOULD BE DISQUALIFIED."
I CORINTHIANS 9:24-27

We visited our local children's science museum a few weeks ago. It is one of those wonderful places where everything is kid-sized, kid-friendly, and kid-appropriate.

In one of the rooms they had large plywood cut-outs of firemen, astronauts, and doctors. All you had to do was stick your head through the "face hole" and you could have your picture snapped as any one of the numerous successful professionals.

It was an eerily accurate picture of our culture. Appearance is more important than reality. Form wins over substance.

Our kids are growing up in the age of microwaves and sitcoms. There is no food that can't be cooked in just a few minutes and no problem that can't be successfully solved in a 30-minute TV time slot. But is that the way real life works?

"Hannah, did you know that our friend Carmen is training to run in the Boston Marathon? She hopes to qualify in order to run next year.

"I thought it would be interesting to know what she will wear when she runs it, so I asked her. Here are all of the things she said that she would need in order to actually run that day. Let's dress you up as a runner as we look at them.

It comes down to training.

"First, she said you need to have these sweat bands around your wrists. That's easy. She said you would also need this sweat band around your head, because otherwise the sweat will run down your face, get in your eyes, and either distract you or actually make you run into another person because you can't see.

"Now let's look at clothes. Put this shirt on. She said that you would want a shirt that is not too tight (that would be embarrassing if you were caught on camera, assuming that you're near the front of the race) but also isn't so big so that it flaps as you run and slows you down.

"Here are the shorts; try them on. She said that you don't want those little nylon shorts because they stick to you when you sweat and that's uncomfortable. But you also don't want something like basketball shorts because, just like the big shirt, it will flap in the wind as you run and actually slow you down.

"We'll use your tennis shoes to represent the really good running shoes that she wears.

"You're ready for one last thing. Do you know what it is? It's your number. When you check in at the tables for the Boston Marathon, they will assign you a runner's number that you wear. I made one that looks kind of like what they would give you. Let's pin it to your shirt. You look ready to go, girl!

"If the Boston Marathon were starting in 10 minutes, could you run it and win? Could you show up dressed this way and take home the trophy? You look like all of the other runners. You probably couldn't win, though. You might not even be able to finish the race.

"Why not? Because you haven't trained! Just dressing the part isn't enough to win the race, is it?

"It is that way in our Christianity, too. The Apostle Paul refers to the Christian life as a race. In Hebrews 12:1, he tells us, *'Run with endurance the race that is set before us, looking to Jesus, the author and perfecter of our faith.'*

"Looking acceptable, knowing the right words, or even showing up at church won't help us win the race. It's not about how we look.

"We could dress for that race and still lose. It's about training. Here's the training manual; it's the Bible.

"Let's agree to train together, so that we can run to win the race set before us."

Date #13

Quiet Times

"LET THE WORD OF CHRIST DWELL IN YOU RICHLY,
TEACHING AND ADMONISHING ONE ANOTHER IN ALL
WISDOM."
COLOSSIANS 3:16

We were still about three miles away when the panic started. It was late; it was dark, all seven kids were with me in the van, and there was not a single sign of civilization for at least three more miles.

It was then that I noticed that my gas gauge, one of those annoying ones that tell you every detail, said, "0 miles of gas left." Oops! I considered the possibility of not telling the kids the situation since I still hoped to limp into the gas station before running out of gas. To be honest, I also hoped to avoid the personal embarrassment that was sure to follow since I was sure that my kids would march straight in and announce to anyone who would listen that Mom had forgotten to watch her gas gauge and almost ran out of gas. After considering all of the possibilities, I decided that the lesson to be leaned far outweighed the probable embarrassment. I called for quiet in the car.

"Kids, we are almost out of gas. We don't even have enough to make it to the gas station on the way home. If we run out, we'll have to call Dad and wait for him to go get a gas can full of gas and then come get us.

"Let's ask God for help. I'm not sure exactly how much gas we have left, but I know that the same God who kept the oil burning in the Menorah for seven days can keep our gas burning for a few more miles! Who wants to pray?"

It was a near miss. We coasted downhill for the last block, with a totally dead car, into the gas station and right up to the pump. What a chance for a lesson! Seize the teachable moment.

"You know, kids, we almost ran out of gas back there. If we had run out, we would be stopped by the side of the road somewhere. We could get out and yell at the car and be frustrated, but we could not make it go any further. Cars are designed to run on gas. They have to have it to keep going. We coasted for the last little bit tonight, but even coasting longer helps when you either lose your momentum or you have to go uphill.

"The same thing applies to our Christian life. What is our fuel? That's right — the Bible. Our fuel is our quiet times, our time in the Word every day.

"Just like a car without gas, we cannot keep going long without it. Oh, we can coast for a little while. But eventually we'll lose our momentum or hit a hill, a battle or trial of some sort, and we'll come to a screeching halt in our spiritual lives.

"Everyone has busy days, gets sick, or is tempted to get distracted for a little while. Then we try to coast; we try to depend on past quiet times or deep times with the Lord to keep us going.

Just like a car, we have to keep filling up spiritually

"Do you remember the story of Joseph in Egypt? God warned him to save up grain in the seven good years so that he would have grain in the seven lean years. God knew the lean years were coming and He made provision for Joseph and his people. Joseph obeyed God and saved grain for the coming drought. It's wise to store while you can. But even God-ordained stores run out. If we depend on a reservoir for too long, the storehouse will run dry.

"Just like our car, we have to keep filling up spiritually. How important is our daily time in the Word of God? It is incredibly important! A casual relationship with scripture guarantees a casual relationship with God.

"Let's agree to try not to coast. Let's hold each other accountable to fill up daily."

Date #14

Real or Counterfeit?

"SO JESUS SAID TO THE JEW WHO HAD BELIEVED IN HIM, 'IF YOU ABIDE IN MY WORD, YOU ARE TRULY MY DISCIPLES, AND YOU WILL KNOW THE TRUTH, AND THE TRUTH WILL SET YOU FREE.'"
JOHN 8:31 & 32

I am sure that I don't need to list for you all of the false things the world holds out to our kids as important. In this age of tolerance, it is essential that our kids know what is true and what is not.

Which do they accept as real? The world's redefined idea of marriage or the Biblical picture of marriage? The world's idea of gender confusion or Biblical manhood and womanhood? They need to know that the truth is found in God's Word; anything else is a shadow, a reflection, a counterfeit.

We love to quote part of the above verse, *"The truth will set you free."* But context is king and we must consider the whole verse. It is only if we abide in His Word that we will know the truth. Then that truth will set us free!

Let's teach our kids the importance of abiding in His Word so that they know the truth and are thereby set free from the bondage of the counterfeit the world has to offer.

"Daniel, I would like to give you a dollar. Would you like one? I have two dollar bills here; you may choose whichever one you want."

One dollar bill is real, one is obviously a hand-drawn bill.

"Why did you choose that one? How do you know that this other one is not real? Have you ever seen this fake one before? You couldn't have because I just drew it a few minutes ago. You've never seen the counterfeit one before, yet you knew it was not real.

Knowing the truth will set us free.

"Did you know that there are specially-trained people who look for counterfeit money? When the Treasury Department trains them to look for counterfeits, they don't show them fake money. They couldn't possibly show them all of the fake stuff out there, could they? Instead, they have them study the real dollar bills until they know them so well that they automatically spot a counterfeit!

"They know it's a fake, because they recognize the real thing. Do you think the world around us sometimes tries to convince us of something that is not true? We can't possibly study all of the false philosophies out there, can we? How can we make sure we recognize them as false?

"That's right, just like the men studying our currency, we need to so know the truth that we automatically recognize the lie.

"John 8 tells us how to do that. If we abide, or live constantly in, the Word of God, then we will know the truth. Knowing that truth will set us free!

"I don't want to believe a lie or accept a counterfeit, do you? Let's study the Word of God together, so that we will know the truth."

Date #15

A Map to the Map

"STUDY TO SHOW THYSELF APPROVED TO GOD, A
WORKER WHO HAS NO NEED TO BE ASHAMED."
II TIMOTHY 2:15

"EVERY WORD OF GOD PROVES TRUE; HE IS A SHIELD TO
THOSE WHO TAKE REFUGE IN HIM."
PROVERB 30:5

As a reward for their diligent study in an art history course,
I had taken two of my daughters to a large, metropolitan city to
actually see some of the pieces of art they had studied. It was one
of those cities where driving a car is not an option; one must master
the public transportation system.

After getting a map of the city from the hotel desk, we set
out to see the city. We soon realized we were in trouble. Wandering
just far enough from our hotel to be seriously lost, we finally figured
out our problem. The map had no compass rose, key, or legend on
it.

We had no idea which direction we were heading or how far
the little one inch measurement on the map would actually be.
Were we walking the equivalent of three city blocks or three miles?

We needed a map to the map.

"Mary Claire, when we were looking for the museum that day, we were seriously lost, weren't we?

"It wasn't that the museum wasn't where it was supposed to be. It wasn't that the museum didn't contain the wonderful riches of art that we wanted to see. And it wasn't even that we weren't trying really hard to find it! Sometimes you just need a map to the map.

"You're starting middle school this next year. Have you noticed that some of the girls have started saying things about each other that may not be very kind? Is God interested in how we use our words? What does He think about it? It's a kind of big question, isn't it? Not many people could tell you from memory everything God has to say about our use of the tongue.

May God richly bless you as you seek to study His Word.

"The problem is not with what God said, or even with our desire to know what He has said. We know that the Bible is our map to wisdom, knowledge and life. We may need a map to the map!

"This book is called an 'Exhaustive Concordance.' The word exhaustive means that it catalogues every word in the Bible, every time it is used.

"Let's look up the word 'tongue' in the concordance. Look at this! This is amazing. The word 'tongue' is used 129 times in the Bible! Our tongues and how we use them must be important to God if he talks about it that many times.

"If we studied all of those verses, we would really know what God wants us to do with our tongues, how He wants us to use and not to use them. We would know what scholars call, 'the full counsel of God' on this issue.

"Everyone needs a map to the map. I actually bought this one for you. In the front I've written a note. It says, 'Dear Mary Claire, I'm proud of the woman after God's own heart that you are becoming. I'm looking forward to studying the 'full counsel of God' together with you for years to come. May God richly bless you as you seek to study His Word.' Then it says II Timothy 2:15, my name and the date today.

"Shall we start working our way down that list on the tongue a few verses at a time beginning tonight?

"We'll learn two great lessons: What God says about the use of our tongues and how to use your new concordance. I'm looking forward to our time together."

Date #16

Stuff-mart

"SEEK FIRST THE KINGDOM OF GOD AND HIS RIGHTEOUS-
NESS, AND ALL THESE THINGS WILL BE ADDED TO YOU."
MATTHEW 6:33

Twentieth century theologian Francis Schaeffer said that within all of us is a God-shaped vacuum, crying out to be filled. Do our kids feel that void, that longing? Absolutely!

What does the world tell them to do with that sense of longing? Fill it with some thing. Add an activity, a hobby, or an object. The problem is that the added thing may distract momentarily; however, it doesn't fill the hole that only God can fill.

We need to teach our kids that although "stuff" is fun, it doesn't satisfy. A trip to "stuff-mart" is never the answer to our heart's cry for a deep relationship with the God who created us.

"Sarah Grace, I want you to do something for me. Close your eyes and think back to three Christmases ago. You would have been 6 years old then. What one gift, one thing, did you want more than anything else? What toy did you talk about and ask for and look at in every ad? Can you picture it in your mind? Do you remember it? Can you see it?

"Now open your eyes. Did you get out of bed this morning and run straight over to that toy and say, 'I can get out of bed and face whatever this day brings because I have this toy?' Did you wake up thinking, 'I am satisfied with life because I got this thing three years ago?'

"No. That thing you wanted so desperately three years ago, that thing that you thought would make you really happy if you could only own it, is now broken and rusted in the garage. Did it make you happy for a short amount of time? Yes. Did it cease to make you happy pretty shortly thereafter? Unfortunately, yes again.

"That is because things were never designed to make us happy. They were never meant to bear that weight or hold up under that responsibility. Things can distract us temporarily, but they can't satisfy us for long. Only God can do that.

"Trying to fill that longing — that hunger — is a problem as old as history itself. As long as there have been people and "stuff," there has been the temptation to try to fill that void ourselves, rather than to go to God.

"Look at Jeremiah 2:13 with me. God is telling the people, His people, why He is disciplining them. They have committed two evils. First, they have forsaken Him, the only fountain of living water ... the only thing that will satisfy.

Do you remember the toy you got three years ago?

"Secondly, they have hewed out cisterns for themselves. Broken cisterns that cannot even hold water. That means they are trying to satisfy themselves with things from their own hands. It won't work, will it? Things from their own hands, 'stuff,' cannot satisfy them. It is useless and empty just like a jar for holding water that has a major crack in it. It cannot do what we want it to do.

"But now let's go to Isaiah 55:1. It is God's invitation to His people. He says, 'Come, everyone who thirsts, come to the waters.' He wants to fill that longing in us.

"'Stuff' will never make us happy for long; it will never satisfy us. Remember that Christmas present in the garage? It only temporarily distracts us from the hunger we have for something greater. Then the hunger and the thirst come back. Let's agree to trust God to fill our longings. Let's remind each other to seek Him first!"

Date #17

It Leaves a Stain

"WITH IT (THE TONGUE) WE BLESS OUR LORD AND
FATHER, AND WITH IT WE CURSE PEOPLE WHO ARE MADE
IN THE LIKENESS OF GOD. FROM THE SAME MOUTH COME
BLESSING AND CURSING. MY BROTHERS, THESE THINGS
OUGHT NOT TO BE SO."
JAMES 3:9-10

Have you ever said something that you instantly wished you could take back? Most of us have made that mistake. Before the words even leave our lips, we realize they were a mistake.

Whoever made up the old rhyme, "Sticks and stones may break my bones, but words will never hurt me," was either a liar or sorely misled.

All choices have consequences. That includes our words! We want to teach our children that words do, indeed, have consequences, sometimes long beyond the moment. Although a heart-felt, "I'm sorry," does wonders, it does not automatically erase all hurt. If our kids can get that concept, hopefully they will choose their words more judiciously.

"Laura, I need to talk to you for a minute. You and I had a disagreement this morning and you said some unkind things to me.

I really appreciated you saying that you were sorry when I told you how badly you had hurt my feelings.

"I want to show you something; I hope we'll learn a Biblical principle from it. I have an old t-shirt here. I know this sounds silly, but I want you to squirt ketchup all over the front. Go ahead, make a pattern on it.

"Now we'll let it sit here awhile, then we'll put it in the washer all by itself. While you finish your homework, I'll wash and dry the shirt."

Later, after washing and drying the shirt.

"What do you notice about it? Yes, you can still see a faint stain from the ketchup. Did I wash the shirt to try to quickly remove the effects of the ketchup? Yes. Did it take a lot of it away? Yes. But is there still a slight stain on the shirt, an effect of the ketchup? Yes.

"Our words are like the ketchup on this shirt. Once they are out and have caused damage, it's hard to make all of the effect go away. When we say we're sorry, it's like washing the shirt. Most of the stain goes away. The hurt feelings, and the slight stain on the relationship, are still there. We can't just wish that away.

Words leave stains.

"Our words have great consequences. I don't want to leave a stain on the soul of someone, so I must choose my words very carefully.

"Just because I think it, I don't have to say it. I want to choose words that bless, not words that curse and leave a stain. Can we both agree to pray that God will give us the self-control and grace to do that?"

Date #18

Chapstick

"DO NOT LET ANY UNWHOLESOME TALK COME OUT OF
YOUR MOUTHS, BUT ONLY WHAT IS HELPFUL FOR
BUILDING OTHERS UP ACCORDING TO THEIR NEEDS,
THAT IT MAY BENEFIT THOSE WHO LISTEN."
EPHESIANS 4:29

It was the opening day of camp. Within a few hours, over a thousand children, youth, and parents would pour through our gates. Although it is an incredibly fun place to grow up, it can also be a rather stressful place. Imagine being a preacher's kid with 18,000 people watching your every move over the course of 11 weeks.

It's easy to get tired of sharing your parents. It's easy to get tired of sharing your home. It's easy to start grumbling and complaining, thinking of yourself instead of the people around you.

We needed a gentle way to remind ourselves to watch our attitudes and our words. We needed a "secret code word."

"OK, guys, what do we need to pray about before we head over to opening day of camp?

"We are going to come in contact with lots of people during the next 11 weeks. It is not just Dad who is in ministry; when God called Dad into ministry, He called our whole family.

"We want our words to be a blessing to all those around us. But sometimes we just forget or get tired and cranky.

"These verses from Ephesians tell us that all of our words ought to be wholesome. That means our words must be three things:

1) they should build others up,

2) they need to be according to THEIR need (not mine), and

3) they ought to benefit all who listen.

"I think we ought to agree to help each other use our words this way. How can we remind each other when we start to use our words in a way that doesn't fit this scripture?

"How about a secret code word? That way we don't have to risk embarrassing each other by correcting each other in public. No one will even know what we are talking about when we encourage each other to live out these verses.

"What word do you want to use? How about the word 'chapstick'?

"What does chapstick do? It heals and soothes. That's what we want our words to do! So whenever we need to remind each other to use our words correctly, we can just whisper 'chapstick' to each other.

"I am excited to see what God is going to do in our lives as we make a deliberate decision to encourage each other to use our words the way He wants us to.

"Let's ask God to help us do that."

Date #19

Life or Death?

"THIS DAY I CALL HEAVEN AND EARTH AS WITNESSES
AGAINST YOU THAT I HAVE SET BEFORE YOU LIFE AND
DEATH, BLESSING AND CURSES. NOW CHOOSE LIFE, SO
THAT YOU AND YOUR CHILDREN MAY LIVE."
DEUTERONOMY 30:19

"A WORD APTLY SPOKEN IS LIKE APPLES OF GOLD IN
SETTINGS OF SILVER."
PROVERBS 25:11

"Just kidding."
"I didn't mean it."
"I was just teasing."
"Duh!"

You might easily have heard all of these when listening in on a conversation between kids. Talk first, think later is probably the norm unless we teach them the importance of words.

Our kids rarely have malicious intent with their words; they simply aren't considering the importance of what they say. The concept we want them to understand? Words, like actions, have consequences.

"Hannah, what do I have here?

"That's right. It's a blender. What does a blender do? It blends things up. It chops them up into tiny pieces. You might even say that it destroys them, right?

"Look what I bought at the pet store this afternoon. Three goldfish! Aren't they pretty?

"I think I'll put them in the blender. There, don't they look good in there? OK, do you want to hit the mix or the frappé button to turn it on now?

"Why shouldn't I turn it on? You're pretty horrified at even the prospect, aren't you?

"You're right. It would be a horribly cruel thing to do. I would never turn on the blender and kill or destroy those beautiful goldfish. I would never willingly choose to hurt or destroy a living creature.

"But have you considered the fact that we are tempted to do something similar every day?

"When I say something unkind about a friend, a family member, or even a teacher, I destroy that person's character. I hurt him emotionally. It's as if I use my words to turn on the blender in his life.

Why are we so willing to hurt each other?

"I would never hurt a goldfish, yet, unfortunately, I am perfectly willing to hurt someone that Jesus Christ made and died for. Someone made in the image of God himself.

"Which is worse, really?

"Why don't you take these cute little guys up to your room? I bought this bowl for them to live in. Every time we look at the fish, let's remember that just like this verse says, we choose life or death with our words.

"Let's ask the Lord to give us the grace to offer apples of gold to all those around us. Even the ones who we think don't deserve it. We don't ever want to be the one to turn on the blender on someone made in the image of God!"

Date #20

The Cost of Lying

"KEEP YOUR TONGUE FROM EVIL AND YOUR LIPS FROM
SPEAKING LIES."
PSALM 34:13

"THERE ARE SIX THINGS THE LORD HATES, SEVEN THAT
ARE DETESTABLE TO HIM: HAUGHTY EYES, A LYING
TONGUE, HANDS THAT SHED INNOCENT BLOOD, A
HEART THAT DEVISES WICKED SCHEMES, FEET THAT ARE
QUICK TO RUSH INTO EVIL, A FALSE WITNESS WHO
POURS OUT LIES, AND A MAN WHO STIRS UP DISSENSION
AMONG BROTHERS."
PROVERBS 6:16-19

What child hasn't been tempted to lie, thinking he will avoid punishment or consequences? Lying is nothing new. We only have two chapters of the Bible before the first lie is introduced in scripture. We have only to go to Genesis 3 to hear the father of lies say, *"Did God not say?..."* as he concocts the first recorded lie.

We want our children to know the high cost of lying.

"Mary Claire, you told me a story yesterday about a girl at school who lied to her mother.

"Why is that a big deal? Why does it even matter that she lied? Why is it important? What's the big deal?

"You are absolutely right. The most important thing is that it doesn't please God. Let's look at these verses from Proverbs 6 to see what God thinks about lying."

After reading the verses.

"That's pretty strong language, isn't it? Not only does it say that He 'detests' and 'hates' lying, it compares it with murder and some other pretty horrible things. Obviously, lying is a really big deal to God.

"When we sin, we tend to think of it as sinning against another person. For example, 'She sinned against her mother by lying to her.' But when David is caught in his sin with Bathsheba, he doesn't say, 'I sinned against Bathsheba or her husband, Uriah,' although that would most certainly be true. He says, 'I have sinned against the Lord.'

"Our sin, any sin, is first and foremost, a sin against God. That's one reason lying is such a big deal.

"There's another issue. Let's look at what lying does to our relationships with other people. When that girl lied to her mother, she caused a relationship of trust to be broken.

"I want you to take this glass and drop it on the concrete out here on the driveway.

"What happened to the glass? It broke into a hundred little pieces, didn't it? Can the glass be put back together? Yes, but it will take a lot of time and effort. You will have to start with the big pieces and work into all of the little pieces. It will take real work.

"That is what we do to a relationship when we lie. We break the trust in the relationship. Just like this glass, the relationship is fractured. And just like this broken glass, it has to be put back together, little by little, with lots of work.

"There is a reason God hates lying. It damages our relationship with Him and with others. God wants what is best for us when He tells us not to lie. I would never voluntarily throw down and break a valuable piece of glass. Let's pray that God will help us not throw down and break our relationships with those around us by lying."

Date #21

State of the Union Birthday Date

"TEACH US TO NUMBER OUR DAYS ARIGHT, THAT WE
MAY GAIN A HEART OF WISDOM."
PSALM 90:12

Politicians love to give "State of the Union" addresses. They know how to capitalize on an annual review of past accomplishments, using it to show us how much progress has been made. They also show us their vision for the future and what they hope to accomplish in the next year. It serves as both a reminder and an encouragement.

We need to do the same thing with our children and their lives. If we are not deliberate, a year can easily pass without focusing on any goals or accomplishments. It is easy to get bogged down in the everyday details and forget the big picture of what we're trying to teach our children. The days do indeed sometimes drag, but the years race. We want to help our kids number their days, that they might get a heart of wisdom!

An annual birthday "state of the union" date is a great way to begin to do just that. At our house each year, that means a breakfast birthday date with Dad. They make their plans the night before, picking any restaurant they want for the celebration. It has become a hallowed tradition that no one wants to miss.

"Happy birthday, Laura. I really treasure this time with you each year. Thank you for letting me take you on a birthday breakfast date. I want to start by telling you how proud I am of you. You are becoming a woman of God, and it's fun for me to watch. I can't wait to see all that God has in store for you as you grow up.

"Let's look at your last year together. Where do you feel like you grew the most? What do you do better today than you did last year at this time? What accomplishments are you most proud of?

"In the movie Chariots of Fire, Eric Liddel says, 'When I run, I feel His pleasure.' What is there in your life that you can say, 'When I do _____, I feel His pleasure.'

"What were some successes you had this past year? What were some failures? Where did you see God's hand in either one?

"I think you had a great year. You really did grow, both physically and spiritually. I'm proud of you.

What did you do this year that made you feel God's pleasure?

"Let's look forward to the next year now. What would you like the next year to look like? What would you like to be better at by this time next year? What new thing would you like to tackle or what existing skill or ability would you like to master? How can your mother and I help you get there? What do you need from us?

"What are you looking forward to in the next year? What are you dreading? How would you like to grow spiritually in the next year? How would you like your mother and I to help you there?

"Is there anything you would like to tell me? Anything you wish Mom and I knew? Anything you wish we would do differently?

"I love you and I am so glad that God gave you to me. You are my favorite 12 year old in the whole world! I'm proud of you and the woman of God that you're becoming. Please, always feel free to come to me during the year to talk about any of these things. I want to be there to help you. Happy birthday!"

Date #22

Diligence

"THE PLANS OF THE DILIGENT LEAD TO PROFIT AS SURELY
AS HASTE LEADS TO POVERTY."
PROVERBS 21:5

What child has not been tempted to hurry and finish something so that they could move on to something more enticing and entertaining? Have you ever told your kids to clean their room, only to find the floor cleared, but most of the items stuffed under the bed? Or asked them to finish their chores, only to find them distracted by some toy halfway through the assigned list?

Within most of us is the tendency to just get it done so that we can cross it off the list. The problem is that our grandmothers told us the truth. I grew up hearing, "Any job worth doing, is worth doing well!"

The issue? A job half done is really not done at all. We want our kids to see this truth. We want them to know the value of being diligent and persevering until it is done.

"It's dinner time kids! Come on to the table.

"Since Dad is out of town, I thought it would be fun to have breakfast for dinner, so we have waffles, and bacon and eggs tonight.

"While the waffles and bacon finish cooking, we'll go ahead and eat our eggs. Here you go kids, eat up.

"What do you mean, you can't eat these eggs? I realize they're not really cooked, but I worked hard here. I took them out of the refrigerator, cracked them open, whipped them, and put them on your plates. I did a lot of the things that are required for serving eggs.

"Can someone tell me what the problem is here?

"You're right — they're not cooked. I didn't finish the job, did I?

"I started the job and I actually did a good part of the work required, but I didn't finish well.

"It's pretty unappetizing, isn't it?

"It's not good or helpful to anyone. Although I spent time on it, it was a waste of my time and yours because I didn't finish the job. I actually made more work for both of us, didn't I?

Let's finish what we start!

"Do you ever give me half-scrambled eggs, kids?

"Remember this afternoon when I asked everyone to do their chores before they went out to play? Remember how I asked everyone to finish their homework before they came to dinner?

"When you got halfway done and then got distracted and quit, you gave me half scrambled eggs!

"It's pretty frustrating to be given half-scrambled eggs, isn't it?

"Let's agree to be diligent before the Lord. To finish what we start. To honor both Him and each other by not giving each other half-scrambled eggs, OK?"

Date #23

Family Devotions

"TASTE AND SEE THAT THE LORD IS GOOD; BLESSED IS
THE MAN WHO TAKES REFUGE IN HIM."
PSALM 34:8

There are a few words that you can say out loud in a Christian audience and you will see almost everyone in the room cringe. The words, "quiet time" will usually bring an uncomfortable silence. The words, "family devotions" bring about outright guilt in most of us.

We all want to have these wonderful, worshipful, life-changing family times, but we end up overwhelmed, discouraged and burnt out. Is it even a realistic desire or a pipe dream? Can we really have our very different age span kids in the same room at the same time and get anything out of family devotions? Can they be something more than a source of frustration for everyone involved?

Perhaps the problem is with our method, not the desire itself.

I love those wonderful family times where you pass out a prop to each one of the kids. Everyone squeezes the toothpaste out of the tube and onto a paper plate. Then you hand them a toothpick and tell them to put the toothpaste back in the tube.

My kids are so competitive that they figured out how to poke a hole in the tube with the toothpick, so that they could then suck up the toothpaste in their mouths and spit it back in the tube.

I spent most of the time praying that one of the little ones wouldn't swallow so much toothpaste that I would have to spend the rest of the night cleaning up from the throwing up!

We then went to the Proverbs to discuss that words are like toothpaste. Once you squeeze them out, it's impossible to get them back in. Exhausting, but it was a great lesson and well learned.

I don't know about you; I don't have the time or the money to spend on elaborate set ups like that. At our house, we call those, "vacation devotions." If I set that as the standard, we only get around to doing them on vacations a few times a year.

I don't want to spend hours a day getting ready for it (because, in reality, I won't) and I don't want to spend large amounts of money buying supplies for it (because I don't have it!). What I really want is for my family to get together three or four times a week to, *"Taste and see that the Lord is good."* I want an easily accomplishable routine for regularly coming into His presence as a family.

"After dinner tonight, we're going to try a new kind of family devotion time together. Your mom and I have been discussing it, and we are convinced that it is really important for us to worship together as a family. But we don't want to make it so difficult that we won't get it done or so time-consuming that we won't get around to it. So tonight we'll try something new. All you need is your Bible. We'll start after we clear the table.

"Welcome to our first official 'Four on the Floor' (Or 'Five Alive,' or whatever catchy name you can come up). We are going to limit ourselves to 20 minutes tonight so that everyone can then get back to homework or whatever else still needs to be done. Can we all agree that we almost always have 20 minutes that we can spare in an evening for something this important?

"Let's start with some singing. Psalm 100 tells us to, *'Worship the Lord with gladness. Come before him with joyful songs.'* So let's start there. The two youngest get to pick the songs tonight and then we'll rotate and take turns picking the songs. That way we'll get to sing everyone's favorite song sometime this week. We don't even need musical instruments, we're making a joyful noise!

"That was definitely a joyful noise. Good job kids. Now everyone grab your Bible and open it to the James, chapter one. I'll read it out loud and we'll talk about what we just read. How does it apply to our lives? What will that look like really lived out in our lives?

"The point of scripture is to bring about changed lives. I don't think we'll ever get more than about four verses covered in any single family devotion, because if we skip any point or application, we're saying that verse doesn't apply to our family. So let's take it apart verse by verse and see what God has to say to us in the next 10 minutes or so. If it takes us all year long to finish James, that's OK. We're not in any hurry.

> **The point of scripture is to bring about changed lives.**

"That was great, guys! Now we want to spend some time in prayer. Scripture tells us that we can boldly approach the Throne of Grace, so let's do that together. It can be hard for the little ones to pay attention when someone prays a lengthy prayer, and we all want to all be active participants as we pray together, so here's how we'll do it.

"We'll follow the acronym ACTS. That stands for Adoration, Confession, Thanksgiving, and Supplication. We'll go around the table and everyone will take turns praying. I'll start and pray two sentences of adoration, then Mary Claire will pray two sentences of adoration, then Hannah, then Laura, and so on all the way around the table. When it comes back to me, I'll start us on the next topic — confession. We'll go all the way around the table each saying two sentences of confession. We'll follow that in the same way with thanksgiving, then end with adoration. Let me explain each one of those words, so that we all know what we're talking about.

1) **Adoration** — We want to adore the Lord, to tell Him how much we love Him. That's not something we're used to doing in our culture, so if you want to use your Bibles and quote some of it back to God, that's great. For instance, if

you want to quote something like Psalm 8, '*O Lord, our Lord, how majestic is your name in all the earth,*' that's fine. Or if you want to simply praise him for some of His attributes, that's fine, too. We'll get better at it as we do it more.

2) **Confession** — We want to confess to the Lord our sins. If you need to stop during it and ask a brother or sister's forgiveness too, that's fine. Matthew 5:23 & 24 tells us, '*Therefore, if you are offering your gift at the altar and there remember that your brother has something against you, leave your gift there in front of the altar. First go and be reconciled to your brother; then come and offer your gift.*' Confession calls us to keep short accounts with each other.

"The goal here is that we want to confess what's really on our hearts, not just what's socially acceptable. We want to avoid always saying something like, 'and forgive me if I did anything that fell short of the mark today, God.' Confession calls us to keep short accounts with God."

3) **Thanksgiving** — Yeah! Here's one we're good at. We'll go around and everyone can thank Him for something specific. We want to find somewhere that we saw His hand, His kindness, His goodness, His mercy today and thank Him for that.

4) **Supplication** — That means to ask God for something. But we want to be careful not to treat God like some cosmic Santa Claus. We're not really asking for things, like a new bike or a ski trip. Here's a challenging question for us. If God answered, 'Yes,' to all of our prayer requests for the last 30 days, how comfortable would we be? How well would work, tests, and sporting events have gone for us versus how much would the kingdom of God on earth have been advanced? It's OK to pray about work, tests, and sports events. However, we want to encourage each other to pray about eternal things. We want to tell God what we want to see Him do in the world.

"By the time our 20 minutes is over and our family devotions are done, the dessert that Mom put in the oven should be ready. We'll have homemade apple pie and then get back to our homework. I'll meet you kids in the family room in five minutes!"

Date #24

Life on Earth Is Not About Life on Earth

"SO WE FIX OUR EYES NOT ON WHAT IS SEEN, BUT ON
WHAT IS UNSEEN. FOR WHAT IS SEEN IS TEMPORARY, BUT
WHAT IS UNSEEN IS ETERNAL."
2 CORINTHIANS 4:18

Everything around us screams for our attention. Jobs, bills, meetings, errands, church duties. In what has been called the "tyranny of the urgent," we give up the critical for the urgent. It simply makes more noise and demands to be heard. More importantly, we give up the eternal for the urgent. It's really easy to get distracted and take our eyes off of that which lasts forever.

Our kids struggle with the same issue. We want to show them that although homework, sports, popularity, or even what college they will get into someday, are all important things, they are not eternal. We want them to put it all into an eternal perspective.

"Joel, I want you to take the end of this roll of toilet paper and slowly and carefully walk all the way to the other end of the front yard with it. I'll stand here and hold the roll on my fingers while you unroll it.

"OK, stop. Can you still hear me? Good.

"I want you to tear off the end square of the long piece that we are holding. That's right, just one little piece. Now hold it up where we can both see it.

"That one piece represents the 70 or 80 years that we have here on Earth. That's all it is. The entire rest of this roll, some unrolled and lots still rolled up, doesn't even begin to show the time that we will spend with God in Heaven. If I had a roll long enough, I could unroll it all the way to the other side of town and it still wouldn't show even a small amount of the time we will spend with Him in Heaven.

The world has a backwards philosophy.

"Life on Earth is not about life on Earth, Joel. That little piece is just preparation for all the rest of this. Everything here is preparation for everything there. It's not about here. It's not about me. It's about Him.

"As much as it seems like this is all there is, I actually have it backwards if I have that philosophy.

"My gifts, my talents, my trials, my victories, are actually all about preparing me for eternity.

"It puts everything in a different perspective, doesn't it? In trials, it keeps us from despair. In good times, it keeps us from thinking that it's about us and what we've earned or deserved.

"Let's make a commitment to try to help each other focus on that which is eternal, on that which really matters and counts. Let's not focus on that one little square, but on the whole rest of the roll!"

Date #25

What's More Real?

"NOW WE KNOW THAT IF THE EARTHLY TENT WE LIVE IN
IS DESTROYED, WE HAVE A BUILDING FROM GOD, AN
ETERNAL HOUSE IN HEAVEN, NOT BUILT BY HUMAN
HANDS."
2 CORINTHIANS 5:1

It's an alien concept. As much as we want our kids to grasp the concept that life on Earth is not about life on Earth, everything in our culture counters that truth. Just do it. Grab the gusto. You only go around once. Have it your way. You deserve a break today.

The seen sure seems more real, doesn't it? But does seeming mean that it is? Obviously, no. We are not trying to manipulate our kids; we are simply attempting to illustrate a life-changing truth.

"Laura, remember how we talked the other day about the fact that life on Earth is not about life on Earth? We unrolled the toilet paper roll and said that the one little square we pulled off represented our 70 or 80 years on Earth, while the long unrolled portion couldn't even begin to represent our time with God.

"It's hard to stay focused on that which is unseen, isn't it?

"It's really easy to get distracted by what we can see and feel and touch and to begin to think that it's the real stuff, the important stuff.

"I want you to do something for me. Reach back and touch the chair you are sitting in. Can you feel it? Yes? Good.

"Now reach out and feel the air. Can you feel it? No? That's right; we can't feel the air.

"Which one of those two things do you need the most? The chair you are sitting in or the air you breathe?

"You're right. We need the air way more than we need the chair! We need that which is unseen way more than we need that which is seen.

You need air ... but you can't see it.

"Let's try one more thing to help us remember this point. Can you make a paper airplane out of this sheet of paper?

"Good airplane! Now, send it flying across the room. Good job. That paper airplane is pretty real, isn't it?

"Here's a question for you. What made that paper airplane stay in the air after you threw it? What made it float?

"That's right — the air. We're back to the unseen. Can the paper airplane do that which it was meant to do without the air? Again, the unseen is tremendously important, isn't it?

"The unseen is eternal; the seen is temporary. Let's keep our eyes on the unseen, the eternal together, OK?"

Date #26

Oven or Microwave

"I PRAY THAT OUT OF HIS GLORIOUS RICHES HE MAY
STRENGTHEN YOU WITH POWER THROUGH HIS SPIRIT IN
YOUR INNER BEING."
EPHESIANS 3:16

"THEREFORE WE DO NOT LOSE HEART. THOUGH
OUTWARDLY WE ARE WASTING AWAY, YET INWARDLY WE
ARE BEING RENEWED DAY BY DAY."
2 CORINTHIANS 4:16

"THE LORD DOES NOT LOOK AT THE THINGS MAN LOOKS
AT. MAN LOOKS AT THE OUTWARD APPEARANCE, BUT
THE LORD LOOKS AT THE HEART."
I SAMUEL 16:7

We've talked about how our culture values the seen above the unseen. The value placed on the outer over the inner is just as strong. Our children need to know that God values their hearts, so that is where He starts. We look at behavior because it shows the true state of a heart. We want to value what He values, a heart after Him.

"Hannah, thanks for coming to the grocery store with me. Having you along turns a task into a fun outing. I really genuinely like your company.

"Look at all of these magazines that they have here. What themes do you see? What are most of them about?

"I see magazines about exercising, about our bodies, about celebrities, about our homes, and lots of magazines about fashion.

"They are all about our outsides, about how we look or appear, aren't they? That's where our society puts the emphasis.

"Let's buy a cake mix while we're here. I want to show you something interesting when we get home."

After you are home.

"Now, we're going to bake two different cakes. The first one we'll bake in the oven; the second one we'll bake in the microwave.

Let's mix the batter and pour half into each of these two pans. Now, put them in to cook.

Society looks at the outside, but God works on the inside.

"I know you're wondering why we took the cake out of the oven five minutes early. It looks done, doesn't it? As a matter of fact, it looks pretty good! From the outside, everything looks right. It looks ready to eat.

"Have you noticed how many times I said, 'looked' while describing the cake?

"Let's cut it and see if appearance is reality here.

"Yuck! It's all mush on the inside. I don't think I would want to eat this piece of cake. Would you?

"It looked OK on the outside, but it was not ready on the inside. Once someone got past the outside and saw the state of the inside the truth was unavoidable. Appearance is not reality! The outside can look good, but what matters is what the inside looks like.

"Think back to all of those magazines that we saw at the grocery store this morning. Which did they all focus on, the outside or the inside?

"You're right, they all focused on our outer selves — our bodies, our clothes, our appearance.

"We took the microwave cake out a few minutes ago. Remember how you said that it didn't look done. It was still a little mushy and soft on the outside? Let's cut it now and see how it is.

"It's done! Do you know why?

"A microwave cooks from the inside out. The inside was done when we took it out; it just took a little longer for it to finish cooking on the outside.

"We are a lot like these two cakes, Hannah. God works on us from the inside out! If we focus on getting the inside, our hearts, done right, the outside will follow.

"If we focus on the outside, we may end up 'looking' all right, but not really ready for anything on the inside. Eventually, something — stress, exhaustion, failure, pressure — will show what we are really like.

"I Samuel 16:7 says, *'The Lord does not look at the things man looks at. Man looks at the outward appearance, but the Lord looks at the heart.'* There is very little in the world around us that encourages us to work on our inner appearance, our heart, more than we work on our outer appearance.

"Let's focus on what God values. Let's agree to ask God to change us for real, from the inside out."

Date #27

A Heart Check

"DO NOT STORE UP FOR YOURSELVES TREASURES ON
EARTH, WHERE MOTH AND RUST DESTROY, AND WHERE
THIEVES BREAK IN AND STEAL. BUT STORE UP FOR YOUR-
SELVES TREASURES IN HEAVEN, WHERE MOTH AND RUST
DO NOT DESTROY, AND WHERE THIEVES DO NOT BREAK
IN AND STEAL. FOR WHERE YOUR TREASURE IS, THERE
YOUR HEART WILL BE ALSO."
MATTHEW 6:19-21

A wise person once said that we judge others by their actions, but ourselves by our motives. We let ourselves off the hook pretty easily, don't we? We say, "I really meant to get that done today, the day just got away from me." We excuse ourselves from responsibility because we knew what we really meant.

It is easy to excuse ourselves spiritually, too. We might be thinking, "God knows that I really love Him; I'm just so exhausted from work that I need to sleep in tomorrow instead of spending time with Him." Or, "God knows that He's my real passion; it's just that right now I'm just too busy to attend Bible Study." Or, " I'll go back to tithing as soon as I have these bills paid off."

Jeremiah 17:9 says, *"The heart is deceitful above all things and beyond cure."*

We want to teach our kids to have an honest "heart check." We don't want them to rationalize or excuse a passion for anything else over Him.

It's easy to see and point out the sin in another person's life. It's harder to be honest with ourselves.

If our kids feel like we're always pointing out their sin, they'll do what most living sacrifices do — they'll crawl off the altar. They need to see us turn God's Word on ourselves and our own lives with a greater intensity than we do on theirs. They need to see us examine our own lives, in light of God's Word, in order to be willing to examine their own.

"Daniel, what do I think about God?

"That's right, son. I love Him with all of my heart. But I read something really interesting today. Want to hear about it?

"I read about how we let ourselves off the hook pretty easily. We get busy and distracted and we start to take God for granted. We assume we're growing as Christians and honoring Him with our lives when really we're all about ourselves.

"I really want my passion to be Jesus Christ. But, unfortunately, it's way too easy to be lulled into letting my passion become personal peace and affluence. That means being comfortable.

"Jeremiah 17:9 says, *'The heart is deceitful above all things and beyond cure.'*

"I can't let my own heart, how I feel about things, and what makes me happy at the moment, be my barometer. I need a 'heart check.'

Can you trust your heart?

"In Psalm 139:23-24, the psalmist says, *'Search me, O God, and know my heart; test me and know my anxious thoughts. See if there is any offensive way in me, and lead me in the way everlasting.'*

"That's what I want. To know if there is anything I need to change so that I pursue everlasting, or eternal, things.

"That means I have to do two things on a regular basis. First, just like the psalmist, I need to ask God to show me my heart.

"Then I need to honestly examine my life. This book I was reading said that we can see where our real passion is if we just look at our checkbook and our calendar. The best indicator of my heart is where my time and my money went in the last month.

"I'm not sure that I like what I saw when I did that. Although I want to *'hunger and thirst after righteousness'* and to seek Him first, I think I have to admit that I have gotten a little too preoccupied with the world.

"Will you pray for me that God will help me to want Him more I want anything the world has to offer and that I would order my calendar and my checkbook to help me pursue that?

"Thanks, Daniel. I appreciate your listening and your prayers. I love you!"

It's in the Scratch

"THEREFORE, I TELL YOU, DO NOT WORRY ABOUT YOUR LIFE, WHAT YOU WILL EAT OR DRINK; OR ABOUT YOUR BODY, WHAT YOU WILL WEAR. IS NOT LIFE MORE IMPOR-TANT THAN FOOD, AND THE BODY MORE IMPORTANT THAN CLOTHES? LOOK AT THE BIRDS OF THE AIR; THEY DO NOT SOW OR REAP OR STORE AWAY IN BARNS, AND YET OUR HEAVENLY FATHER FEEDS THEM. ARE YOU NOT MUCH MORE VALUABLE THAN THEY? WHO OF YOU BY WORRYING CAN ADD A SINGLE HOUR TO HIS LIFE?"
MATTHEW 6:25-27

Today demands our attention. If we're not careful, it begins to command our affection as well. The temptation to get totally caught up in the events and significance of today and to think that this is what really matters is very real to both ourselves and our children.

No matter how good or how bad the events of the moment are, we must continually remind ourselves that life on earth is not about life on earth. We must learn to look beyond this temporary moment to that which is eternal.

It was a rainy Wednesday afternoon. Because I was sched-uled to speak to a group of parents that day, I had asked my 16-

year-old son to pick up his 10- and 12-year-old sisters from their gymnastics workout in town.

An incredibly cautious driver, he had slowed down because he knew the streets would be slick because of the rain. As he rounded the last curve in the road before the gym, a stalled car blocked the road. Although he pumped the breaks on his 1967 pickup, it was in vain. As if in "super-slow-mo" from an Olympic telecast, he hydroplaned into the stalled car.

As we discussed it late that night, he was still horrified at the whole event.

"Mom, this was the worst day of my life! I did everything I could have done to avoid that accident, but there was no way I could stop it. Just think what might have happened if the accident had happened five minutes later on my way home instead of on the way there. Mary Claire and Hannah would have been with me and they might have been badly hurt. I would never have been able to forgive myself if that had happened!

The here and now seems so BIG, but it's really quite small.

"There was no way I could stop in time even though I was going 10 miles slower than the speed limit. The policeman was walking around the curve to put up cones to warn people of a stalled car, but he hadn't had time to get there and put them up yet. Because I hit the stalled car, I got the ticket for failing to yield.

"Now to avoid having my insurance go up, I'm going to have to pay to get that man's car fixed out of my savings. I have been saving for college for four years and the whole thing is about to be wasted fixing some other guy's car from an accident I couldn't avoid!

"I now have to start all over again saving for college, I don't have a car that drives anymore, and the girls might have been badly hurt. This has been the worst day of my life!"

It was my turn to talk.

"Will, I know this has been a very hard day. I am so sorry for all that has happened to you. I feel terrible for what happened to you. I would change it all if I could.

"I am proud of you for driving cautiously today. I know that you were doing everything you could have done to avoid that accident. And you did all of the right things after you had the accident. You showed real integrity in the way you handled it. The man you hit told your Dad that he was impressed with how you conducted yourself today — that you acted like a man, not a 16-year-old boy.

"There are lots of times when we don't like how life turns out. Things happen that we don't think are 'fair' or that we don't deserve. Sometimes we get the rare privilege of seeing why God allowed something to happen in our lives, but lots of times we're left wondering and having to simply trust Him.

"If the Bible is true, and it is, then everything that happens to us is for our good and His glory. You've seen me do needlepoint. If you look at the back of the fabric, all you see is knots, tangled threads and an unrecognizable picture. But when you get to see a glimpse of the front, you see a beautiful tapestry beginning to take form.

"That's the way it is with our lives. God is making a beautiful picture, but we can't always see it yet.

"Take this ball of twine and let's unroll it. Take your end and go stand way over there on that side of the family room. Now I'm going to take this pen and make a tiny little scratch mark somewhere in the middle of the piece of unrolled twine.

"Can you see the tiny little scratch mark from over there where you're standing? It seems pretty inconsequential from way over there, doesn't it? It's not really a big deal when you look at the whole ball of twine, is it? But when you're right there in the scratch, it seems huge.

Life is more than cars, money, and college.

"That scratch represents our lives. That scratch is your crummy day. It's my hard year. It seems at the time like it's all there is. But when you look at that scratch compared to the whole ball of twine, it's small. When we view our days in light of all of eternity, there's a way bigger picture.

"We have to keep it all in perspective, Will. We focus so much on the scratch that we begin to believe that it's all there is. We build scratch careers, scratch relationships, even scratch lives.

"I don't want to build my life based on a mere scratch. I want to build it based on eternity.

"I know that today was a crummy day, dear. I know you could drive yourself crazy with all of the 'what-ifs?' But it's in the scratch, buddy. I know you've got some hard work to do now to climb out of this, but don't let it steal your joy.

"Life is more than cars and money and college. Life on Earth is not about life on Earth. There's a much greater theme and purpose. Let's not get stuck in the scratch. You handled yourself well, today, as a man of integrity. I love you, buddy."

Date #29

A Turtle Lesson

"BUT THIS ONE THING I DO: FORGETTING WHAT IS BEHIND AND STRAINING TOWARD WHAT IS AHEAD, I PRESS ON TOWARD THE GOAL TO WIN THE PRIZE FOR WHICH GOD HAS CALLED ME HEAVENWARD IN CHRIST JESUS."
PHILIPPIANS 3:13B-14

"CHILDREN, OBEY YOUR PARENTS IN THE LORD, FOR THIS IS RIGHT. HONOR YOUR FATHER AND MOTHER — WHICH IS THE FIRST COMMANDMENT WITH A PROMISE — THAT IT MAY GO WELL WITH YOU AND THAT YOU MAY ENJOY LONG LIFE ON THE EARTH."
EPHESIANS 6:1-3

In the heart of all kids lies this question: Why should I obey? They may be the wonderfully easy, compliant, kind of child or they may be the push every button and test every limit kind of child. They have been taught the concept of obedience since they were toddlers. But why? Any lesson learned without the "why" behind it has to be questioned at some time. Without knowing the principle behind the command, it is hard for it to generalize to a life lesson.

Do our kids need to obey? Absolutely! Do they need to learn the concept of first time obedience even when they don't understand why or don't agree? Absolutely!

But if we can help them learn a principle in the meantime, the lesson will be much easier learned and reinforced.

"Sarah Grace, it's time to feed 'Herb,' our turtle. Will you bring him to me, please?

"I'm just going to hold him here in my lap while you and I talk for a few minutes. Then we'll go into the kitchen and find him a nice, fat strawberry. How was your day?"

Since God knows what is best, why don't we just trust Him?

As I am talking, I am holding the turtle in my lap. Sitting on the ground over carpet, so as not to let the turtle get hurt, I let him walk right off my lap as we are speaking.

Sarah Grace has been taught by her brothers that a turtle who falls on his back can't get up easily and may die. As Herb falls with a clunk, she cries out in alarm.

"Mommy, why did you do that to Herb! Pick him up quickly or he'll die!"

"Why did I do what, honey?"

"Why did you drop him?"

"Sarah Grace, I didn't do anything to Herb. I simply held him in my lap. He got impatient and walked off of my lap all by himself. I didn't push him; he did it all by himself.

"I would have protected him had he stayed here. I know everything he needs and provide it all for him. As a matter of fact, I was getting ready to feed him his very favorite thing in just a few minutes. I have his best interests in mind and know way better than he does what is truly best for him.

"We are like that with God sometimes. He holds us in His hands and knows what is best for us. He provides everything we need. Yet we walk right out of his lap and fall when we disobey Him.

"It was silly for Herb to walk off of my lap, wasn't it? He should have stayed in the hands of his caretaker. It would have been better for him.

"If you obey, you choose to stay in the loving, protecting hands of your creator and caretaker. Let's pray right now that God will help you to always choose to stay in His hands, that you will choose to obey!"

Date #30

Don't Fly the Coop

"OPEN MY EYES THAT I MAY SEE WONDERFUL THINGS IN YOUR LAW. I AM A STRANGER ON EARTH; DO NOT HIDE YOUR COMMANDS FROM ME. MY SOUL IS CONSUMED WITH LONGING FOR YOUR LAWS AT ALL TIMES. YOUR STATUTES ARE MY DELIGHT. THEY ARE MY COUNSELORS."
PSALM 119:18-21 & 24

"HE REPLIED, 'BLESSED RATHER ARE THOSE WHO HEAR THE WORD OF GOD AND OBEY IT."
LUKE 11:28

Rugged individualist. Self-starter. Independent. Free thinker.

If you asked the average American kid to list attributes he or she thinks would describe a successful person, you would probably hear all of these. Because our culture tends to value these characteristics, we think of them as highly desirable attributes.

What about obedient? Talk about "milk-toast!" Would our kids even put that characteristic on the same list? If our culture doesn't value obedience, we need to show them that God does.

The saying in our house is, "Obedience brings blessing, disobedience brings pain." It's a Biblical principle! Let's show them how it works.

One of the easiest ways to teach kids Biblical principles is in nature. God has built His principles into all of His creation. It's easier to learn a costly lesson second hand from nature, then make it applicable to our own lives.

Whether you live in the city or the middle of the country, nature provides ample teaching opportunities. We just have to learn to look for them and then use them.

We had recently moved to the country and had decided that it would be fun to get a few chickens. It sounded so sweet and picturesque to imagine our little ones heading out to the chicken coop every morning to pick up the fresh chicken eggs. I thought it would be a fun lesson in "where does our food come from?" but God had a much greater lesson in store for us.

We went to the local feed store to buy a dozen baby chicks. A naive city dweller all my life, I asked if we could just take them home and let them go in the backyard. After the man at the feed store finished laughing at me, he sold us all of the paraphernalia we would need to successfully raise our cute little chicks until they reached egg-laying maturity.

At this point I already had way more money in this endeavor than I had ever imagined. I figured our chicks would have to lay about 50 dozen eggs each before we ever broke even. But we were in this for the lessons, not the economics. This was one of these moments when my husband, Mario, would say through gritted teeth (only somewhat resembling a smile), "We're making memories, right?"

As soon as the chicks were big enough to be let out of their homemade incubator in the garage, we joyfully loosed them in the yard to become "free range."

It took only a few days for the Golden Eagle who had a nest in one of our pine trees to discover his new neighbors. What we called "free range," he called "free buffet!" We watched in horror as our uninvited guest swooped down every other day and helped himself to the tasty buffet morsels we had so thoughtfully provided for him.

Determined to save our remaining flock, my husband and boys headed back to the feed store to get instructions on how to build a chicken coop.

With $50 more in building supplies, they began construction on what fondly became known in our household as "the chicken Taj Mahal."

This was the chicken coop to end all chicken coops. It was such an amazing structure that my little kids wanted to know if they could have slumber parties in this coop. We had chicken wire, aluminum siding, a tin roof, a leveler for straight posts, even a door!

As we began work on the coop, we closed the remaining chickens in the garage until we could once more guarantee their safety. When the four posts were set in concrete and the wire fencing secured to them, we moved the chickens out to the coop as we continued work on it.

Rules are here to protect us.

With continuously fresh water, a five gallon container of organic corn, shade from the scorching East Texas sun and fresh straw for comfort, this was truly the chicken Taj Mahal! We knew exactly what these chickens needed to thrive and we had provided it all.

But even as we finished building and stocking everything, one chicken, Harriette, spent her every moment trying to escape. She constantly ran between our legs. When the door to the coop was left open, she ran straight out. Before the roof was installed, she hopped over the walls. She was one continual escape attempt.

After a long day's work of successfully finishing the coop and caging all of the chickens, we went in for the night.

The next morning my kids ran out to check the status of their beloved chickens after their first night in the Taj Mahal. Horrified, they ran in to tell me that there was one less chicken than there should be. Harriette was nowhere to be seen.

We began a search party for the missing Harriette. Unfortunately, it took only a few minutes to discover her. Or more succinctly, what was left of her — a beak and a few feathers. She had fallen prey to the most common predator in our area — a coyote.

What I really wanted to do at that moment in time was to quickly hide the evidence and announce that she must have escaped and was happily living somewhere else. But there was a lesson to be learned here. Sadly, I called the children over to my discovery.

"Kids, I need you to come see what I found here. It's all that is left of Harriette. I know this is terrible, but there is a very important lesson to be learned here.

"We knew exactly what Harriette needed. We provided everything she needed not just to survive, but to thrive. We gave her food, water, shelter, a safe environment, companionship, love — everything she needed. But she was sure that there was something better outside the coop. Remember how she spent all day yesterday trying to escape?

"What we provided for her for safety, she saw as us keeping her from the good stuff. What we provided as protection, she saw as withholding. She was sure that it would be better outside the coop.

"When she went outside the coop, she gave up our protection. The coop was there to protect her. When she stepped outside of it, she left herself vulnerable to the coyotes. Because there was no longer anything to protect her, a coyote got to her and destroyed her.

"Sometimes it gets frustrating to follow the rules that Dad and I have put in place in our home, doesn't it? But our rules play the same role in our lives as the chicken coop did in Harriette's life. The rules are there to protect us.

"It can seem like the rules are keeping us from having fun. It can seem like there is something better out there if we didn't have the restraining existence of those rules in our lives. But every one of our rules is based on what God says is best for us. He knows everything we need and has provided it for us.

"When we seek to step outside the rules or break them, we leave ourselves vulnerable, just like Harriette did. Harriette would have been better off had she trusted the hand of her master. It is the very same for us, guys.

"Let's learn a lesson from poor Harriette. When we chaff at the rules, let's remember that our master really does know best and has our best interests in mind. When we step outside the rules, we step outside God's protection. Let's not make ourselves willing victims for the coyotes of the world. Let's agree to remind each other that the rules are there to protect us, the provision of a loving Master who knows what's best."

Audience of One

"BUT WHEN YOU GIVE TO THE NEEDY, DO NOT LET YOUR LEFT HAND KNOW WHAT YOUR RIGHT HAND IS DOING, SO THAT YOUR GIVING MAY BE IN SECRET. THEN YOUR FATHER, WHO SEES WHAT IS DONE IN SECRET, WILL REWARD YOU."
MATTHEW 6:3-4

"BUT WHEN YOU PRAY, GO INTO YOUR ROOM, CLOSE THE DOOR AND PRAY TO YOUR FATHER, WHO IS UNSEEN. THEN YOUR FATHER WHO SEES WHAT IS DONE IN SECRET, WILL REWARD YOU."
MATTHEW 6:5

"BUT WHEN YOU FAST, PUT OIL ON YOUR HEAD AND WASH YOUR FACE, SO THAT IT WILL NOT BE OBVIOUS TO MEN THAT YOU ARE FASTING, BUT ONLY TO YOUR FATHER, WHO IS UNSEEN; AND YOUR FATHER, WHO SEES WHAT IS DONE IN SECRET, WILL REWARD YOU."
MATTHEW 6:17-18

Since it was only an hour until dinnertime, I had told the boys that there would be no more snacks until Grandma had dinner ready. It was now eerily quiet in the house. I walked into the living room and asked, "Will, Joel, where are you?" After about a 10-second pause, Will answered, "We're not behind the curtain eating Oreos, Mom."

The "seen" seems real and the unseen seems like it doesn't really exist. We begin to buy into the philosophy that if no one sees us, it either didn't happen or it doesn't matter. But what our kids need to begin to learn is that there is no such thing as "getting away with it." That which is a secret sin on earth is an open scandal in Heaven. Our Heavenly Father does indeed see all! We really do perform for an audience of One.

We all perform for an audience of One.

We were driving down a two-lane country road near our home when I committed the unpardonable sin, according to the driver behind me: I drove the speed limit. After weaving back and forth for almost a mile, waiting for a chance to pass me, the angry man roared past us. Red-faced and shouting, he shot us an obscene gesture as he passed.

"Mom, was that man waving at you?" my 6-year-old asked. "Do you know him? He seemed really mad about something!"

Now I have to explain this to my children in a way that will be OK when they, in turn, tell every child they talk to this week.

"No, I don't know that man, kids. But you're right, he did seem very angry! The gesture that looked like a wave was a very unkind way of him expressing his anger toward us. We don't ever want to treat another person that way.

"He was angry with us because he was speeding and we were in his way. We were slowing him down."

"Why was he speeding, Mom?" asked Hannah.

"Because he thinks he won't get caught, sweetie. He thinks that because there is no policeman in the area, he can break the law and not have any consequences. What he doesn't understand is that there is someone way more important than a policeman watching him.

"He doesn't know that we perform for an audience of One. God sees everything we do. That man thinks that he 'got away with it.' But there is no such thing as 'getting away with something.'

Actions have consequences. He will learn someday that discipline deferred does not mean discipline denied. That which is a secret sin on earth is an open scandal in Heaven.

"I would imagine that someone with that much anger in his life doesn't know Jesus Christ personally. Let's take a minute and pray for that guy. Let's pray that God will protect him and all of the other drivers around him. And more importantly, let's pray that God will send someone to tell him about Jesus.

"What do we need to learn from this man, kids?

"That's right, we want to remember that we perform for an audience of One. And that audience of One matters way more than any audience here!"

Date #32

Actions Matter

"THEN THE KING WILL SAY TO THOSE ON HIS RIGHT,
'COME, YOU WHO ARE BLESSED BY MY FATHER, TAKE
YOUR INHERITANCE, THE KINGDOM PREPARED FOR YOU
SINCE THE CREATION OF THE WORLD. FOR I WAS HUNGRY
AND YOU GAVE ME SOMETHING TO EAT, I WAS THIRSTY
AND YOU GAVE ME SOMETHING TO DRINK, I WAS A
STRANGER AND YOU INVITED ME IN. I NEEDED CLOTHES
AND YOU CLOTHED ME, I WAS SICK AND YOU LOOKED
AFTER ME. I WAS IN PRISON AND YOU CAME TO VISIT ME.'
THEN THE RIGHTEOUS WILL ANSWER HIM, 'LORD, WHEN
DID WE SEE YOU HUNGRY AND FEED YOU, OR THIRSTY
AND GIVE YOU SOMETHING TO DRINK? WHEN DID WE SEE
YOU A STRANGER AND INVITE YOU IN, OR NEEDING
CLOTHES AND CLOTHE YOU? WHEN DID WE SEE YOU SICK
OR IN PRISON AND GO TO VISIT YOU?' THE KING WILL
REPLY, 'I TELL YOU THE TRUTH, WHATEVER YOU DID FOR
ONE OF THE LEAST OF THESE BROTHERS OF MINE, YOU
DID FOR ME.'"
MATTHEW 25:34-40

"He started it!"
"She did it first!"

"I'm not helping her, she was mean to me yesterday!"

It seems to be our natural inclination to give people what they deserve. But there are two problems with that philosophy. First, we're giving them what WE think they deserve. We tend to judge ourselves based on our motives and others based on their actions. We let ourselves off of the hook pretty easily, because after all, we know what we meant to do, whether or not we actually managed to do it.

How we view others is an entirely different matter. They, after all, ought to get what they deserve! It seems only "fair." They started it, did it first, let us down, or dropped the ball.

Perhaps my judgment or opinion on what someone deserves ought not to be the standard. My perspective might be slightly skewed. Jeremiah 17:9 says: *The heart is deceitful above all things and beyond cure.* Maybe my heart is not the best arbiter of justice.

That leads us to the second problem with giving people what they deserve. It's not a Biblical principle! The Biblical principle is not to give people what they deserve, it's to give them what we would give Christ himself, if He were here. If we treated everyone around us the way we would treat Christ, might that change the way our families interacted? Absolutely! Let's examine the difference between treating someone the way they deserve versus treating them the way we would treat Jesus.

"Sarah Grace and Daniel, I need you both to come here for a minute.

"Sarah Grace, I know you're mad at Daniel because he took your new ball away. You just got it for your birthday yesterday and it's very special to you. But even though he took your ball, hitting him is not the right way to respond.

"Daniel, I know you're frustrated with Sarah Grace for not sharing with you. She's been playing with her new ball all day and you've been asking for a turn. But grabbing it out of her hands is not the right way to respond.

"Let's have a family meeting. I want us to read a part of the Bible together. Let's read Matthew 25:34-40. I'll read it out loud and you guys listen.

"Sarah Grace, if Jesus were here right now, would you share your ball with Him? Of course you would! You would want to share

113

it with Him. I want you to think about the Bible passage we just read out loud. Jesus is not physically here in this room right now. But when you share your ball with Daniel, it is just like you shared it with Jesus, Himself. In some amazing way that I don't really understand, it is credited to you as having shared it with Jesus! So when you share with Daniel, you share with Jesus! You actually do get a chance to share your new ball with Jesus.

"It's not about whether or not Daniel deserves a turn with your new ball. It is your ball. That's not the issue. The issue is that according to the Bible, when you share with Daniel, you share with Jesus.

"Daniel, if Jesus were here right now, would you grab something out of His hands? Of course not! That's a horrifying thought, isn't it? But according to these verses, when you grab something out of your sister's hands, it is just the same as grabbing something out of Jesus' hands.

"Again, it's not a question of whether Sarah Grace was sharing or not. She wasn't! It's not a question of what she deserves. The question is, 'How would you treat Jesus?'

Would you share with Jesus? You would wait respectfully for Him to finish, wouldn't you? When you treat Sarah Grace with patience and respect, it is credited to you as having treated Jesus, Himself, that way.

"You may never get a chance to share your new ball with Jesus or to treat Him with patience and respect. But when you do that for anyone around you, the 'least of these,' it is doing it for Jesus.

"That's an exciting thought! You really do get the chance to share with Jesus or to do something for Him.

"It works that way with our words, too. Sometimes we say things to each other that we would never say to Jesus. But whatever we say to each other is credited to us as what we say to Jesus, Himself! We want to watch our words very carefully and make sure that we speak to everyone around us, the 'least of these,' the same way we would to Jesus.

"It is always exciting to learn something new from the Bible. Unfortunately, we have short memories and tend to forget, or grow complacent about, what we have learned. We really want to help each other live out what we've learned. So let's come up with a way to remind each other of this amazing truth.

"When we see each other treating someone in a way we wouldn't treat Jesus, we'll whisper, 'Would you treat Jesus that way?'

"And if we're talking to someone else in a way we wouldn't talk to Jesus, we'll whisper, 'Would you talk to Jesus that way?'

"I want to give you guys permission to remind me of this, too. Hopefully, we'll hold each other accountable to treat each other and speak to each other, not as we think someone deserves, but as we would Jesus.

"I think that's pretty exciting. What about you guys? I'm really proud of you for wanting to know what the Bible says about how we treat others and for wanting to live it out. I love you!"

Date #33

Just an Irritating Sibling?

"AS IRON SHARPENS IRON, SO ONE MAN SHARPENS
ANOTHER."
PROVERBS 27:17

"He's bugging me!"

"She's driving me crazy!"

"Mom, make her get out of my room!"

If you ask almost any parent what one thing most
disheartens them about parenting, they're likely to answer, "sibling
rivalry." It is incredibly discouraging when our kids argue, squabble,
and drive each other (and us) to distraction.

If we're honest, we would probably all admit to occasionally
being frustrated by someone in our lives. But how do we look at
that frustrating, irritating person? How do we train our kids to view
that person? If God is, indeed, sovereign over everything, then that
includes irritating siblings! God is not capricious; there must be a
reason. But how do we explain it to our kids?

"Mary Claire and Hannah, I want to show you something.
Come look at what I have in my hands. In this hand, I have a piece

of charcoal. In the other hand, I have my diamond ring. If I were to offer to give you one or the other, which one would you want?

"You're right. I don't know anyone who would take the charcoal over the diamond. The diamond is both beautiful and valuable. But there is something interesting about the diamond.

"The diamond began as charcoal! Heat and stress and pressure acted on it and caused it to go from a hunk of coal to a beautiful gem. Although I'm sure it wasn't pleasant at the time, I'd say that was a pretty good trade, wouldn't you? It was worth it.

"I know this sounds a little odd, but that's what I want for you girls. For you two to turn out to be beautiful gems. Do you know what the heat and stress and pressure are in your lives? To some extent, it's each other!

"Scripture calls it iron sharpening iron in Proverbs. I know that sometimes you girls drive each other crazy. I want to challenge you to look at it a little differently. Maybe instead of just being a bother, it's really all about God's mercy and love in your life.

We sharpen each other, and that is a beautiful thing!

"What seems like an irritation to you is really God using a sister to sharpen you, to turn you from a lump of coal into a beautiful diamond. Maybe it's not about the sibling at all and instead about what God wants to do in your life!

"If that's true, then having an irritating sibling goes from being a bother to being an instrument of God. The fact that you have a sister who drives you crazy shows how much God loves you! He's not willing to leave you as a lump of clay.

"So the next time your sister drives you crazy, ask God to help you see it as His love. He's using that pressure to turn you into a beautiful diamond!"

Date #34

Rubbing Off the Rough Edges

"FOR OUR LIGHT AND MOMENTARY TROUBLES ARE
ACHIEVING FOR US AN ETERNAL GLORY THAT FAR
OUTWEIGHS THEM ALL."
2 CORINTHIANS 4:17

All of us have rough edges. Few of us like to have those edges rubbed off. It's not that we don't like the end result; it's just that the process is rather painful. Pain is not something that we normally seek or enjoy.

God quite often uses those closest to us to rub off those rough edges. One of my favorite books on marriage is Gary Thomas' *Sacred Marriage*. I really love the subtitle: "What if God designed marriage more to make us holy than to make us happy?"

What if God designed relationships, usually siblings when we're young, to rub off our rough edges? It's all in the semantics. Kids call it "bugging me." Adults call it sanctification!

"Boys, I have a project for you. I want you to take this pile of rocks and make a wall with it. See how solid and sturdy you can make it. I'll come back and check on your progress in a few minutes.

"It's pretty hard to make it functional, isn't it? As soon as you get about three rocks high, it starts to teeter and falls over.

"What would make the rocks stay where you put them so that you could actually make something useful out of them? You're right — their shape would have to change. They won't lie flat shaped like they are right now.

"But if I take them and knock off all of their rough edges, if I use them to grind each other's rough spots off, then I can stack them up and make a wall that will last. Now the rocks have served two purposes. They were used to make each other useful and they made a wall that serves a purpose, is beautiful, and will last.

Cutting off the edges makes us useful.

"Look at the pictures of beautiful stone walls in this book by James Herriot. Aren't they great looking walls? They're sturdy and beautiful and useful. But they started as piles of rocks that had to be shaped in order to work together.

"If I took this pile of rocks and banged them together to knock off the rough edges it would produce heat and maybe even some sparks. But the end result would be rocks that could be used in a wall like this. That's what you boys are doing for each other. You are rubbing off each other's rough edges.

"The issue is with how you view it. You can look at each other and say, 'He drives me crazy.' Or you can look at it and say, 'God loves me so much that He is using my little brother to knock off my rough edges so that He can make something beautiful of my life.'

"I know it's hard to look at the irritations in your life as showing God's love. But I'm proud of what you boys are becoming. God is using you in each other's lives. I can't wait to see what He does in you and through you!"

Date #35

Second Servings &
Second Place

"YOUR ATTITUDE SHOULD BE THE SAME AS THAT OF
CHRIST JESUS: WHO, BEING IN VERY NATURE GOD, DID
NOT CONSIDER EQUALITY WITH GOD SOMETHING TO BE
GRASPED, BUT MADE HIMSELF NOTHING, TAKING THE
VERY NATURE OF A SERVANT."
PHILIPPIANS 2:5-7

A heart that really desires to serve those around them. It's what we all want to see in our kid's lives. Talk about counter culture! From self-serve gasoline to self-serve seating to self-serve ice cream, we live in a "serve yourself" kind of world. An alien concept just a few generations ago, the very word "self-serve" has become part of our culture.

Being willing to serve others is not something that will just happen. A habit of the heart must be developed and practiced the same way any other habit would be. Any way that we can give our children practice in being a servant is invaluable.

Who is the hardest person to serve? A sibling!

If we can train our kids to serve each other, it will be much easier for them to serve others later. Let's give them an easy, consistent way to practice!

"We're going to start a new tradition tonight, kids! We want to learn to serve others, just like Jesus did. But we'll have to practice it for awhile before it really becomes a habit.

"Do you remember when you learned to ride a bike, Will? It took lots of practice before you could do it without having to think about every step. Finally it became a habit and was much easier to do. We want to begin to train our hearts toward the habit of service.

"Here is what we're going to do. From now on, whenever anyone wants seconds on something at a meal, he will first offer to get seconds for anyone else.

Learn to serve others.

"So if Will wants more soup, he'll say, 'I'm going to get more soup. May I get anyone else more of anything?'

"If we're at McDonald's and Will wants a refill on his drink, he will offer to refill everyone else's drinks first. Do you think he might have to make two or three trips to the fountain before he actually refills his own? Probably so. But it is great practice serving others.

"I know it's just a little thing, but it's a beginning. If we can cheerfully serve each other, it will be much easier to serve those outside our family. We want to begin to train our hearts toward a life of service. Unfortunately, being selfish is easy; I am looking forward to watching God start to give us a heart that desires to serve others. It's a habit I want to learn!"

Date #36

Secret Service Agents

"BUT WHEN YOU GIVE TO THE NEEDY, DO NOT LET YOUR
LEFT HAND KNOW WHAT YOUR RIGHT HAND IS DOING,
SO THAT YOUR GIVING MAY BE IN SECRET. THEN YOUR
FATHER, WHO SEES WHAT IS DONE IN SECRET, WILL
REWARD YOU."
MATTHEW 6:3

OK, I'll serve others, but I want some praise for doing it! I want to hear what a great Christian kid I am. I want everyone to know how sacrificial I am in my actions.

Few of our kids would actually articulate those sentiments, but unfortunately, many feel exactly that way. What we've succeeded in building into our kids is a performance-based service ethic.

Let's be honest; we all love praise! As nice as it is, we want to remember that we perform for an audience of One. The goal here is to give our kids a chance to serve while not letting their left hand know what their right hand is doing. A chance to serve in secret — a chance to learn the joy of serving for that audience of One.

"Sarah Grace, I have a fun game for us! You are going to be a Secret Servant Agent today. Your target is your big sister, Laura.

She has a lot of tests in the next few days and has been studying really hard. We want to find a way to be a blessing to her.

"But here's the catch. We want to be a secret blessing! The Bible tells us that when we do good works, or acts of kindness, we don't want our left hand to know what our right hand is doing. I know that sounds a little confusing, but what it means is that we want to do it in secret, if possible. We want to do it because when we serve others around us, we are really serving Jesus Christ.

"It's nice when someone notices that we've done something and says, 'Thank you.' Most people really like to be thanked. But we want our reward for serving to be a Heavenly reward, not an earthly one. You remember how good it felt when everyone applauded after your ballet recital? We want to learn to seek the applause of Heaven, not of men.

"That is not the way we normally think, so we'll have to practice doing things without any recognition. But God gave you a great way to practice when He gave you brothers and sisters.

"We'll start with Laura this week, because she's having such a hard week. What nice thing can you think of that we can secretly do for her? She is taking a shower right now and getting ready for school. What if we silently snuck down the hall and made her bed and straightened her room for her? That way she'll have a few more minutes to study before she leaves for school.

Serve others secretly ... and see what happens!

"When she asks who did it, I'll tell her that A Secret Servant Agent did it and that he or she wants only the applause of Heaven! She'll feel honored that someone cared enough to be a blessing and you will have gotten the privilege of serving the Lord by serving someone around you.

"I think we ought to try to be a Secret Servant at least once a week. I'll assign different people to serve each other every time. It might be that you get someone, like Laura, who is having a difficult week. Or, if you've been arguing with a brother or sister, that is a perfect person to find a way to serve. It takes your focus off of your 'rights' in the argument and puts it on honoring them.

"I can't wait to see what great things God does as we learn to serve each other with no goal of recognition or thanks. I think it will be really fun to watch Him work in each of our lives and in our family. Who do you want to serve next week? I'm proud of you for being willing to serve God by serving others!"

Date #37

Special Friends

"DO NOTHING OUT OF SELFISH AMBITION OR VAIN
CONCEIT, BUT IN HUMILITY CONSIDER OTHERS BETTER
THAN YOURSELVES. EACH OF YOU SHOULD LOOK NOT
ONLY TO YOUR OWN INTERESTS, BUT ALSO TO THE
INTERESTS OF OTHERS."
PHILIPPIANS 2:3-4

Recently, our family had the privilege of staying at a four-star resort. My husband was speaking at a conference there and our whole family had been invited along as guests. With nine of us, we don't tend to stay in a lot of hotels at all, especially four-star ones! My kids were, as my grandmother would have said, "in hog heaven."

Every time one of them would call the front desk for anything (which they found ample opportunity to do) the clerk would end the conversation with, "Is there anything else we may do for the Zandstra family?"

I would quickly hear, "Mom, this is great! I love it here! Can we come back sometime?"

It did feel great to be at that fabulous hotel. We all love to be served. It comes naturally to us. What doesn't come quite so naturally is the desire to serve others. We are good at "looking out for number one." What we want to encourage our kids to get good at is looking out for the interests of others. It's a rather sad truth that the hardest people for our kids to serve are their family members. But a child who can learn the habit of serving a brother or sister can much more easily serve wherever God calls him later in life. Let's use that to begin to train a heart of service.

Serving each other is one very visible mark of a Christian.

"Family meeting in five minutes, kids. We're going to start something new that I am really excited about. Meet me in the living room.

"Who liked being at that wonderful hotel last week? Wasn't it great? Tell me what you liked about it? That's a great list, I think you all thought of just about everything.

"People come to that hotel from all over the world. It's a very famous hotel. Do you know why? I can tell you in one word what makes them stand out — service. They specialize in serving their guests. It really felt great to be served that way, didn't it?

"Serving each other is supposed to be one very visible mark of a Christian. Listen as I read this passage from Philippians 2. We all naturally look out for our own interests. But these verses tell us that we are also supposed to look out for the interests of others. That's not quite as natural, is it?

"When Hannah learned to play tennis, how did she get so good at it? That's right, by practicing. We want to get good at serving, or looking out for the interests of others. The way we will do that is by practicing.

"In order to encourage us to practice serving, we are going to assign 'special friends.' Everyone will have a special friend to whom they are assigned. Your job is to look for ways to serve that person. You are looking for ways to look out for their best interests.

"For example, Will, your special friend this month will be Sarah Grace. It will be your job to put her in and out of her car seat when we go anywhere. You can sit beside her in the car and read her little books or hand her toys to keep her happy. If she needs a refill on her drink at dinner or drops something at the table, you can get it for her. Your job is to find as many ways to serve her in any given day as you can. As you serve her, someone else will be serving you!

"We'll keep our 'special friend' assignments for a month so that we can really begin to get good at looking out for the interests of that other person. Then at our family meeting next month, we'll decide whether we want to switch 'special friends' or keep the same ones for a longer period of time.

"I think we'll be amazed at how much God begins to develop a heart of service in us simply because we are obedient to try to do it. I really think He will do great things in us and through us. Let's end our family meeting by praying and asking Him to enable us to look to the interests of those who are around us. I'm proud of you guys for being willing to try this. I love you!"

Date #38

Family Prayer Partners

"AGAIN, I TELL YOU THAT IF TWO OF YOU ON EARTH
AGREE ABOUT ANYTHING YOU ASK FOR IT WILL BE DONE
FOR YOU BY MY FATHER IN HEAVEN. FOR WHERE TWO OR
THREE COME TOGETHER IN MY NAME, THERE AM I WITH
THEM."
MATTHEW 18:19-20

It is hard to remain angry at someone when you pray with them. I distinctly remember learning that lesson as a young married woman. Mario and I had just disagreed completely on what we would do. It escalated into a disagreement on almost every front. After reaching a frustrating stalemate, he said, "I think we had better stop and pray about this right now."

After being on our knees together before the Throne of Grace, two things happened. First, I felt pretty petty about my part in the disagreement. Secondly, I had trouble remembering what I had been so angry about.

As Matthew says, *"Where two or three come together in my name, there I am with them."*

Will our children someday have serious disagreements with their spouse, family members or boss? Most likely, yes. Did our children probably have a serious disagreement with a sibling today? Most likely, yes. Their relationships today are actually the perfect training ground for the adult relationships of tomorrow. If we can teach them to take their disagreements, together, to the Lord, they will be much better equipped to handle those later, more weighty disputes in a Godly manner.

"Where two or three come together in my name, there I am with them."

"Hey kids, as soon as we've finished doing the dinner dishes, I want us to visit together for about five minutes. Let's meet in the living room.

"Any time two or more people live together, there will be disagreements. Even as believers, we all tend to see things differently. It is way too easy to let a disagreement turn into an argument.

"I am seeing a tendency to argue starting to develop in our family. We know that's not what the Lord wants for our relationships. When we argue, it's usually over our own personal preferences, agendas, or desires. It shows that we've forgotten, at least

Practice inviting God into our relationships.

for the moment, the lesson we learned from Philippians 2:3-4 about considering one another's interests above our own.

"So what do we do when we notice that we've started to argue or quarrel or complain about someone or something? The answer is to invite the Lord into the situation. And the way to do that is by prayer.

"Matthew 18: 19-20 tells us that, *"Where two or three come together in my name, I am there."* That's exactly what we want and need in our relationships, especially when we are in disagreement.

"We want to practice doing that very thing, inviting Him into our relationships. So starting tonight, we are going to have prayer partners. I'll assign a partner to each of us. Our job is to spend about five minutes together in prayer after dinner each night. A good way to start would be to ask each other what they want prayer for. Then we'll spend a few minutes praying out loud for each other.

"As odd as it sounds, if there is anyone we are having a disagreement with, we want that person to be our prayer partner for the week. We want to invite God to change that relationship. We want to ask God to help us see that person as He sees them. It is really hard to stay angry at someone we're praying with.

"Dad and I will assign the prayer partners every Sunday night. Let's begin tonight! The greatest tool we have to work out disagreements with other Christians is prayer and the greatest place we have to learn it is right here in the safety of our family.

"Let's ask God to help us keep short accounts, an eternal focus, and right relationships in our family as we begin to pray regularly with each other."

Date #39

Revenge

"DO NOT REPAY ANYONE EVIL FOR EVIL. DO NOT TAKE
REVENGE, MY FRIENDS, BUT LEAVE ROOM FOR GOD'S
WRATH, FOR IT IS WRITTEN: 'IT IS MINE TO AVENGE: I
WILL REPAY,' SAYS THE LORD."
ROMANS 12:17A & 19

It is a no-win situation. You can hear the yelling and arguing from a block away. As you enter the room, you've entered the parental "twilight zone," but it's more aptly called "the argument zone."

"She started it!"

"I did not, he started it!"

"She took my toy."

"No way; he hit me."

Most parents spend the next few minutes dutifully trying to unravel the "who started it?" question so as to know which potential offender to punish. We know our kids pretty well and can usually, with a fair amount of accuracy, guess who actually started the whole fray. But does it really matter?

All we have to do is guess wrong one time and we have lost the battle. If the issue is not just stopping a behavior, but changing a heart, and we pick the wrong "side" (which is how they see it), we now have one child gloating because he got away with it and one child sulking because she was wrongly accused. Neither one is going to learn a lesson that will change a heart.

Although it goes against conventional wisdom, I would like to propose that it really doesn't matter who started it. Both hearts need a readjustment.

"Laura and Will, I need you both to come over here and sit down. Let's talk about what is going on here. You guys got into a pretty strong argument last night, didn't you?

"Have you ever seen part of a hockey game, kids? Sometimes they get in fights during a game. One guy makes an unfair or maybe an overly aggressive play and the other guy now has to decide what, if anything, he is going to do about it. He has to make a choice. He can skate away and the other player may or may not get penalized depending on whether the referee saw the offending behavior or not.

Figuring out "who started it" isn't even the question.

"He can take off his gloves and throw them down. He can decide to fight back. Now did the second guy start it? Absolutely not. He was wronged, offended. But the minute he takes off his gloves and decides to fight back, the referee will penalize both of them. It doesn't matter who started it, they will both spend time in the penalty box, because they both deliberately chose to get involved in the fight.

"In the past, when you two argued, I would have asked you both questions about who started it and that person would have been punished. But we really want God's Word to be the authority in our lives, and I've realized that there is a Biblical principle here.

"Let's read Romans 12:17-19 together. What does this passage tell us about our responsibility when someone wrongs us, or is evil to us?

"Do you know the definition of revenge? The other person was clearly wrong. Just like the hockey player, they wronged someone. But just like the second hockey player, the wronged person now has to decide what to do with the offense. The Bible clearly says that it is our responsibility not to take revenge, not to repay evil for evil. We trust God to come to our defense and to teach that person the lesson that they quite clearly need to learn.

"It is just as wrong to take revenge, or repay evil for evil, as it is to start the argument. The Biblical principle is to return kindness for evil.

"Do you remember the Old Testament story of David and Saul? David had done nothing wrong to Saul, but Saul, along with 3,000 of his men, was hunting David down to kill him. David and his men were camped out in the back of a cave when Saul and his men entered the same cave. While Saul was sleeping, David's men urged him to defend himself, to take revenge. They even told him that it was obviously God's will for him to take revenge since he had delivered Saul into his hands.

"They said, 'This is the day the Lord spoke of when he said to you, I will give your enemy into your hands for you to deal with as you wish.'

"David chose not to take revenge and kill Saul. Instead, he cut off a corner of Saul's robe to show him that he could have taken revenge had he chosen to. The Bible tells us that later David was sad that he had even cut off a corner of Saul's robe.

"Later, in I Samuel 24, David confronts Saul and says, '*This day you have seen with your own eyes how the Lord delivered you into my hands in the cave. Some urged me to kill you, but I spared you: I said, I will not lift my hand against my master, because he is the Lord's anointed. See, my father, look at this piece of your robe in my hand! I cut off the corner of your robe but did not kill you. Now understand and recognize that I am not guilty of wrongdoing or rebellion. I have not wronged you, but you are hunting me down to take my life. May the Lord judge between you and me. And may the Lord avenge the wrongs you have done to me, but my hand will not touch you.*'

"Do you see the same Biblical principle here, kids? The principle is that, as believers, we return kindness for evil. We trust God to avenge.

"So it really doesn't matter who started the argument, does it? We have to make a choice as to whether we will be like that hockey player and throw down our gloves and return evil for evil. Or will we be like Saul and return kindness for evil?

"From this point on, I will not ask you who started the argument. Just like both hockey players are penalized, both persons who choose to get involved in an argument will be disciplined. To take revenge is just as wrong in God's opinion as to start the argument.

"It's hard to return kindness for evil! Let's take a minute and ask God to help us treat each other the way He has told us to. He wants to help us live a life that is pleasing to Him. Let's pray right now."

Date #40

M&M Family

"TWO ARE BETTER THAN ONE, BECAUSE THEY HAVE A
GOOD RETURN FOR THEIR WORK; IF ONE FALLS DOWN,
HIS FRIEND CAN HELP HIM UP. BUT PITY THE MAN WHO
FALLS AND HAS NO ONE TO HELP HIM UP! ALSO, IF TWO
LIE DOWN TOGETHER, THEY WILL KEEP WARM. BUT HOW
CAN ONE KEEP WARM ALONE? THOUGH ONE MAY BE
OVERPOWERED, TWO CAN DEFEND THEMSELVES. A CORD
OF THREE STRANDS IS NOT QUICKLY BROKEN."
ECCLESIASTES 4:9-12

The busyness in our culture breeds a sense of competition even in our families.

"You went to her game last week, it's my turn now."

"She got to go last time, it's not fair."

"He always gets to go first."

We want our kids to have a sense of "family." We want them to root for each other and to see our families as interdependent units, not competing individuals. We want them to see the wonderful blessing God gave us when He gave us a family. There is strength in standing together and efficiency in working together. We learn those lessons in a family!

"Family meeting time, guys! I've got a fun experiment for us to try. Who, besides me, really loves M&M chocolate candies? OK, Joel, you get to be the one to eat M&M's. But first there is a condition. You have to do it a specific way.

"Hold your arms straight out in front of you. I am going to tape these yard sticks to your arms with masking tape. Are they on good and firm? Can you bend your arms at all? No? Good.

"I have a big bowl full of M&M's. Doesn't it look delicious? I'll put it right here in front of you on the coffee table and you may eat all of them that you want! Yum, they look great, don't they?

"What do you mean you can't eat them? Why not? You can't get them in your mouth? Can you pick them up?

"That's interesting. You can pick them up, but you can't get them into your mouth. You can get the job started, but you can't successfully finish it.

"Can you think of any way that you could get those M&M's into your mouth. What might you need?

"Let me offer one additional piece of information. God has already given you what you need to be able to do this. Here is a hint. You don't have to do it alone.

You need help from others, and you need to help others. It goes both ways.

"That's right, you can get help from any of your brothers or sisters. Now does it become easier to accomplish your goal? You can hold the bowl, but they can actually put them in your mouth. Now it's way easier to eat those M&M's, isn't it?

"You couldn't accomplish your goal alone. You needed help in order to succeed. That's one of the reasons God gave us families — so that we might come alongside each other and help each other. That which was impossible on our own can be done when we work together.

"It is way too easy to get busy and to forget to look for ways to help each other. But God wants us to look for ways to be a blessing to each other and to work together as a family. Just like Joel couldn't get the M&M's on his own, God didn't mean us to 'go it alone' in this family. That's why He gave us each other.

"I have a challenge for us. Let's see how many ways we can find during the next week that we can come alongside each other and be a blessing to each other. We'll keep track of them on the refrigerator in the kitchen. Every time you work together, are a blessing, or are blessed by a family member, write it down. At our family meeting next week, we'll read it out loud and celebrate all of the ways God has used us in each other's lives. Who wants to celebrate with M&M cookies?"

Date #41

A Useful Pot

"CONSIDER IT PURE JOY, MY BROTHERS, WHENEVER YOU
FACE TRIALS OF MANY KINDS, BECAUSE YOU KNOW THAT
THE TESTING OF YOUR FAITH DEVELOPS PERSEVERANCE.
PERSEVERANCE MUST FINISH ITS WORK SO THAT YOU
MAY BE MATURE AND COMPLETE, NOT LACKING
ANYTHING."
JAMES 1:2-4

It's a dirty word in American Christianity — suffering. No one wants to use it, much less experience it. But suffering is a reality that cannot be ignored and plays a necessary role in our sanctification as it conforms us to the image of Christ.

From loss of a grandparent to loss of job to health issues to persecution at school, our kids confront suffering from a young age. Any of us who are honest will admit that at the time, it hurts. How do we put it in perspective for our kids? It's an abstract subject that we must somehow begin to make concrete so that it makes sense to them.

It's one thing to rather glibly say, "It will all work out in the end, dear." It's quite a different thing to begin to give them an understanding that even though suffering hurts at the moment, God is in control and He will use it for our good and His glory.

"I have an art project for us today, kids! I went by the craft store earlier and got some terracotta clay. (If terracotta clay is too difficult to find, you can use any modeling clay.) We're going to make pots, like the ones we put our flowers in out on the front porch. Here's a piece for each of you. Let's see how pretty a pot we can each make.

"Great pots, kids! They are really good looking. Now we will set them aside to dry while we have lunch. We'll check them again then to see how they look."

A few hours later.

"OK, so our pots are dried. Let's go look at them. Who can tell me what the purpose of a pot is? What is their function? You're right, the purpose is to hold something.

"If we were to use them to hold a plant, they would have to be able to hold water also. A plant has to have water. Let's see if they can hold water. We'll pour about a cup of water into each one and see what happens.

"Uh-oh! The pots are actually absorbing the water and starting to get mushy again and melt. They looked all right, but they really weren't ready to function, were they? They cannot yet do what they were designed to do.

"Look at this pot that I bought at the store when I picked up the clay. Isn't it gorgeous! It's good and hard and solid and the outside is beautifully painted in this Oriental pattern. I would have to say that, unfortunately, this pot is much more functional and much more beautiful than the ones we made. Would you agree?

"Do you know what the difference is between this pot and ours? This pot started out exactly like ours — it was a hunk of clay. Then someone molded a pot out of that clay, just like we did with our clay. At that point, it was brown and would still melt had someone poured water into it, just like ours did. But now this pot works; it is useful and beautiful. Why?

"There is one major difference in our pots and this one. After this one was crafted, the craftsman put it into the fire. It was so hot in that fire that the pot almost melted, but it didn't. Instead, it came out firm, hard, and ready to be used. Then the master craftsman could paint a beautiful picture on this pot that would last forever. The paint won't melt and run.

"In order to go from terracotta clay to a beautiful vase, this pot had to go through the white hot heat of the furnace. The master craftsman knew exactly what the pot needed in order to become a masterpiece. Only a fiery furnace could burn out all of the impurities and make this clay into a really useful, beautiful porcelain vase.

"There is a fiery furnace in our lives, too, kids. It's called suffering. God uses suffering to burn out all of the impurities in our lives and turn us into a firm, useful, beautiful masterpiece. Only after going through the fiery furnace could this vase do what it was created to do and bring glory to its master. But if given the choice, do you think the vase would have chosen to have been put into the fire? Probably not!

Nobody signs up for suffering ... but it's so good for us!

"We are the very same way. Few of us would choose to go into the furnace of suffering. But it is there that we are refined and made into what we were created to be. It is there that we become something that can bring glory to our maker.

"Can anyone tell me somewhere that they are suffering right now? How about in the last year or so? Those are great examples. It is easy to look at suffering as just inconvenient or hard or pain. If we remind ourselves that suffering is really purposeful refining at the hand of a master craftsman, it helps us keep it all in perspective as we find ourselves in the fiery furnace of suffering."

Date #42

Beethoven's Fifth

"BUT WE ALSO REJOICE IN OUR SUFFERINGS, BECAUSE WE KNOW THAT SUFFERING PRODUCES PERSEVERANCE; PERSEVERANCE, CHARACTER; AND CHARACTER, HOPE. AND HOPE DOES NOT DISAPPOINT US, BECAUSE GOD HAS POURED OUT HIS LOVE INTO OUR HEARTS BY THE HOLY SPIRIT WHOM HE HAS GIVEN US."
ROMANS 5:3-5

"Mom, I'm just so disappointed, I wish I could die!"

My sweet daughter had been seriously let down by someone she had respected as an older Christian. She was hurt, embarrassed, and angry. "How could she act like that? She was so mean to us. I just want to cry! How can she call herself a Christian? Either Christianity is not really true, or she's not really a Christian."

It is incredibly painful to watch our children be disappointed. But we all go through it at different times in our lives. The difficult lesson is to learn to keep our eyes on Jesus, the author and perfector of our faith, rather than on those still in the process of being perfected.

"Come in here and join me, Joel. I know you've had a really tough week. It's hard to be disappointed by someone you respected spiritually. Just sit down on the couch and relax. I want to play

141

something on the piano for you. I think this is the most beautiful piece of music ever written; it is by one of the most brilliant composers who ever lived, Ludwig Beethoven. It's called 'Beethoven's Fifth.'

After clinking away at the keys.

"How did you like it? What do you mean is this some kind of joke? I was really trying to play Beethoven's Fifth! Was there a problem?

"OK, I'll be honest here. It probably sounded absolutely horrible, didn't it?

"But here is the issue, Joel. The problem was not with the music, was it? The problem was with the ability level of the person playing the music. The fact that I am a crummy pianist doesn't mean that Beethoven's Fifth is not one of the most amazing pieces of music ever written.

"We see this truth lived out almost daily in our Christian lives. People around us stumble, fall, disappoint us, embarrass us. It's especially hard when it's people who are in positions of spiritual leadership; they ought to know how to 'play that piece.' They should know better.

Never let others keep you from what is true.

"But remember how I said that the problem was not with the music itself, but with my ability to play it? It's the same way in our Christian walk. A person who 'messes up,' no matter how badly, doesn't invalidate the truth of God's Word. The problem is with the messenger, not the message. Don't ever let your discouragement with the musician convince you that the music and its author are less worthy of your praise."

Date #43

A String Bikini

"THESE COMMANDMENTS THAT I GIVE YOU TODAY ARE
TO BE UPON YOUR HEARTS. IMPRESS THEM ON YOUR
CHILDREN. TALK ABOUT THEM WHEN YOU SIT AT HOME
AND WHEN YOU WALK ALONG THE ROAD, WHEN YOU LIE
DOWN AND WHEN YOU GET UP. TIE THEM AS SYMBOLS
ON YOUR HANDS AND BIND THEM ON YOUR FOREHEADS.
WRITE THEM ON THE DOORFRAMES OF YOUR HOUSES
AND ON YOUR GATES."
DEUTERONOMY 6:5-9

We had gone to College Station, Texas to move our eldest daughter into her new freshman dormitory at Texas A&M University. With six younger siblings in tow (ages 15, 13, 10, 9, 6, and 3) we checked into the only hotel near the campus that also had an indoor swimming pool and hot tub. Now the pain of giving up their big sister could at least be partially forgotten by an evening of soaking in a hot tub.

The big kids had their bathing suits on and were out the door before I could even find the floaties for the littlest one. They were excited; this was going to be the highlight of the day.

As we got on the elevator to go to the ground floor and the pool, we met the boys coming back up.

"You know what, Mom, let's just play some games and hang out in our room tonight. We don't need to go to the hot tub."

I know something was wrong! Either that or the pod people had come and sucked their brains out and replaced them with someone else's while I wasn't looking. These were not kids who would willingly give up the thing they had been waiting for all day long.

"Let's go on down and see what's going on, guys," I said.

"Yes, ma'am," they replied, with long faces.

As we rounded the corner to the pool and hot tub area, I saw two women in the hot tub. One was a mother, about my age. Having obviously forgotten her bathing suit, she was swimming in her gym shorts and a white t-shirt. It was a **Being better than someone else is no help to them.** "wet t-shirt" contest in front of our very eyes. Her daughter, a 17 year old who was trying out for the A&M soccer team, was wearing a string bikini.

Worst of all, four empty beer bottles sat between the two of them as they belted down the last two in the six pack. They were so inebriated, they were having trouble talking.

We stood, mouths hanging open, as we looked at the scene before us.

"Family meeting around the corner, kids!" I announced.

We convened, mouths still agape, out of sight of the two women. "Kids, I would assume that these two ladies do not know Jesus Christ. This is absolutely heartbreaking. We need to stop and pray for them right now. We want to pray that God will send someone to tell this mom about Jesus Christ and what He has done for her. She needs someone to come alongside her and teach her how to be a mom to her kids.

"This poor girl needs to hear how much she is loved by God. We need to pray that someone will speak truth to her, and that she will be able to hear it, before she goes off to college. Otherwise, she will have four more years of baggage that she will take into her adult life with her. They need to be spared from themselves. The heart of God is broken-hearted for people like this. Who wants to pray for them?"

144

After we prayed for them, we went on into the pool and hot tub. Because of the immodest attire, the boys, whose Dad had taught them to "bounce," avoided the hot tub and swam in the pool instead. Did we get to share the gospel with them that night? No, they were not even sober enough to have focused and listened to us.

But what we did get to do was practice the right thing to do when we slam into an unbelieving culture around us. The only response is a broken-hearted prayer.

It's not, "They are pagans; I am good. Aren't I glad that I am better than them?"

Instead, it's, "There, but for the grace of God, am I. Oh God, please spare them!"

Date #44

A Bright-Eyed Checker

"DO EVERYTHING WITHOUT COMPLAINING OR
ARGUING, SO THAT YOU MAY BECOME BLAMELESS
AND PURE, CHILDREN OF GOD WITHOUT FAULT IN A
CROOKED AND DEPRAVED GENERATION, IN WHICH
YOU SHINE LIKE STARS IN THE UNIVERSE AS YOU
HOLD OUT THE WORD OF LIFE."
PHILIPPIANS 2:14-16

In line at our local Target store, we waited somewhat
patiently while the checker replaced, for the third time, a cash
register tape that kept breaking. The man in front of us in the line
voiced his frustration loudly and caustically. After what seemed like
an eternity later, we finally paid and left the store.

As we got in the car, we had the following discussion:

"That was hard to wait in line for that long, kids. I'm proud
of you for being patient and waiting without fussing or whining.
That man in front of us in line never learned that lesson, did he?
Everyone around us noticed how impatient and irritable he was.

"But do you know what else I noticed? Our checker. Did anyone else notice the tiny little cross necklace she had on? Not everyone who wears a cross knows Jesus Christ personally. For some people, it's just a piece of jewelry. But I think that girl is a believer.

"Do you want to know why I think she is? She stayed amazingly calm while her cash register malfunctioned and that man fussed at her. She returned kindness for evil and refused to talk unkindly back to him. She did a hard job without complaining or arguing. That is a hard thing to do in that situation.

"She also had a beautiful smile and eyes that twinkled. I think she knows that life on earth, even when it's at its most irritating, is not about life on earth. She had a good perspective on all that was going on around her. She was a blessing even when others around her chose to be a curse.

"I would bet that girl knows Jesus! It showed in her smile, her eyes, and her behavior. She has a hard job. Who wants to pray for her right now? Let's pray that Jesus will be very real to her and that He will continue to help her be a blessing to everyone she comes in contact with in her life. We want to pray that He will continue to do mighty things in her and through her.

Under pressure, may good come out.

"It's a pretty cool thing, isn't it? It's cool to think that someday, someone might be watching one of you kids. And they will know, just by how you react and behave in a hard situation, that you know Jesus Christ! That girl really showed us how to live out Philippians 2:14-16. It says, 'Do everything without complaining or arguing, so that you may become blameless and pure, children of God without fault in a crooked and depraved generation, in which you shine like stars in the universe as you hold out the word of life.' That is exactly what she did today. She shone like a star as she held out the Word of life — the Gospel — to everyone around her. Talk about a witness! Let's pray for her. And let's pray that God will help us to do that same thing to those around us."

Date #45

Good Choices

"THIS DAY I CALL HEAVEN AND EARTH AS WITNESSES
AGAINST YOU THAT I HAVE SET BEFORE YOU LIFE AND
DEATH, BLESSINGS AND CURSES. NOW CHOOSE LIFE, SO
THAT YOU AND YOUR CHILDREN MAY LIVE AND THAT
YOU MAY LOVE THE LORD YOUR GOD, LISTEN TO HIS
VOICE, AND HOLD FAST TO HIM."
DEUTERONOMY 30:19-20A

Sarah Grace was weeping, inconsolably. "But I want to go to Kristen's house to watch a movie!"

"We already discussed this, sweetie. You had to clean your bedroom before lunch if you wanted to be able to go over to her house."

"But I'll clean it now. It's not fair; I want to go!" she cried.

"Sarah Grace, you know the saying at our house. Bad choice, bad ...."

"Consequence," she mournfully finished the sentence.

"That's right, sweetie. Bad choice, bad consequence. I'm sorry that you made a bad choice and now have to live with a bad consequence. Next time, please choose wisely."

Teaching our children how to make Godly choices is one of the most important things we do. We've got to give them a paradigm for how to make a decision that is based on something other than emotions, feelings, or momentary consequences.

Then we have got to give them enough practice making Godly decisions that it becomes a habit. Do you remember the old adage, "Practice makes perfect?" Practice itself only makes a habit, it does not necessarily "make perfect." Only perfect practice makes perfect!

To do this well means we have to do three things.

First, we have to give them that paradigm on decision making.

Secondly, we have to take them on our decision-making journey, inviting them along so that they can see how we make decisions, getting practice second hand.

Thirdly, we need to put them in situations where they can get lots of practice making smaller decisions long before the huge decisions of life have to be made.

"Sarah Grace, come sit down and talk to me. How was your day? What was the best thing that happened to you today? What was the worst?

"I'm sorry, sweetie, I know that you were really disappointed that you didn't get to go over to Kristen's house. But that was your choice, wasn't it? Remember, bad choice, bad ....

"That's right, bad choice, bad consequence. Making good choices is a really big deal in life. I know lots of grown-ups who never learned how to make good choices and they still routinely have to live with the bad consequences in their lives because of their bad choices. You will be making choices all of your life: who to choose as friends, what classes to take, what sports to **Bad choice, bad consequences.** play, how to spend your time, then later, where to go to college, what to do with your life and who to marry. Those are some pretty big choices, aren't they?

"Would you like to learn a set of steps to follow to help you make Godly decisions? Good choice, dear! Let's walk through them together. Do you remember our friend, Kirby Anderson? He is with a wonderful ministry called Probe Ministries. I got these off of the Probe Ministries website (www.probeministries.org). Let's look at their 'Six Steps to Good Decision Making.'

"There are six things we want to consider when we are making a decision. If God wanted decision making to be easy, He could have given us an exact list of everything we would need to know for our entire lives. But He didn't. Decision making is difficult by design! God uses it in our lives to develop our faith. But He does give us some Biblical principles to use in that decision making process. What do we look at when making a decision?

1. **The Bible** — Has God already spoken on this matter? If He has, then the choice is simply whether or not I will obey! I Corinthian 4:6 says: *'Do not go beyond what is written.'* If God has clearly defined the fence, then outside the fence is outside the will of God. If God, in the Bible, has already spoken on this issue, then it becomes an issue of obedience or disobedience.

2. **Prayer** — If we've searched scripture, but the Bible hasn't spoken on the matter, the next thing we need to do is pray about it. We are still going to the author of all wisdom to ask for wisdom. Philippians 4:6 says, *'Do not be anxious about anything, but in everything, by prayer and petition, with thanksgiving, present your requests to God.'* As much as I might desire to know God's will on something, His desire is even greater that I know it. It's not like a cat and mouse game and I'm trying to trick God into telling me the answer. He wants me to know His will. John 16:24 says, *'Ask and you will receive, and your joy will be complete.'*

3. **The Holy Spirit** — I've searched scripture, prayed, and still don't feel like I am ready to make a Godly choice. What do I do next? I listen for the Holy Spirit. He is described as counselor, convicter, comforter, converter, encourager;

aren't those some of the very things I need? But there is an issue here. So far I have diligently searched for the answer, for guidance in a decision. But if I talked to you all of the time and never got quiet and listened to you, could I really know how you felt about something? Not really. We are really good at talking and not very good at listening. To listen requires silence on my part. We desperately need to practice that with God. Psalm 46:10 says, *'Be still and know that I am God.'* How often are we still before Him? In our culture, probably not often. We want to hear what scripture describes as the 'still, small voice of God.' That means I need to pick a time and place where I am quiet and still enough to hear a still, small voice. Romans 8:27 says that, *'the Spirit intercedes for the saints in accordance with God's will.'* I need some planned, intentional silence to listen to the Spirit of God.

4. Conscience — I've read, I've prayed, I've listened. Now, how do I 'feel' about it? But here is one huge warning. The conscience makes a great stop sign, but a terrible green light. Just because I have a clear conscience doesn't mean it is truth. Unfortunately, it is pretty easy for us to sear our conscience. Jeremiah 17:9 says, *'The heart is deceitful above all things and beyond all cure.'* I can trick myself into believing a lot of things if I want them badly enough. So if I 'feel' like God is telling me 'no' to something, then I should accept that answer. But if I 'feel' like my answer is 'yes,' then I need to continue checking it out according to the rest of these things and not just accept it because I feel good about it. You'll save yourself a lot of pain if you remember that the conscience is a great stop light, but a poor green light.

5. Circumstances — We tend to think that circumstances are things that just happen to us. My favorite definition of circumstance is that it is the hand of God in the midst of time. The God who is sovereign over all of creation ordains our circumstances! There is no such thing as chance or luck. Acts 17:26 tells us that, *'From one man he made every* nation of men, that they should inhabit the whole earth; and he determined the times set for them and the exact places where they should live.' God clearly set the circumstances of their lives. That tells me that I ought to look at the circumstances of my life to help me discern the will of God in my life. But you'll notice that it is the fifth thing I consider, after I have considered the other four first.

6. **Counsel** — Now we come to the last thing we consider in making a decision. Godly counsel. We tend to turn that around and have it be the first thing we do. We ask others what they think. It is OK to seek Godly counsel, but we want to do it last — after we have looked at scripture, prayed, listened for the Holy Spirit, looked to our conscience, and checked our circumstances.

"Proverbs 15:32 says, 'Wisdom comes from many counselors.' After we've followed all of these other steps, we're ready to hear the opinion, either agreement or disagreement, of the saints who best know us.

"Sarah Grace, you will be making decisions all of your life.

> **Eventually, decision making will be a natural process, but it takes work to make it a habit.**

Lots of grown-ups still tend to make decisions based on emotion or how they feel at the moment. I want you to be able to make decisions based on scriptural principles. Like we said when we started this discussion, bad choice, bad consequence. Deuteronomy 30:19 says, 'I have set before you life and death, choose life that you may live.'

"My goal is for you to pick some place that you need to make a decision every month for the next year. Then we'll go back over these steps as you seek to practice making decisions from a Godly perspective. Eventually, you'll run through these steps automatically whenever you need to make a decision. You'll be way ahead of most grown-ups by then! I'm proud of you for wanting to learn how to make a Godly decision. What decision shall we start on first?"

Date #46

Truth or Consequences?

"BUT IF SERVING THE LORD SEEMS UNDESIRABLE TO YOU, THEN CHOOSE FOR YOURSELVES THIS DAY WHOM YOU WILL SERVE, WHETHER THE GODS YOUR FOREFATHERS SERVED BEYOND THE RIVER, OR THE GODS OF THE AMOR-ITES, IN WHOSE LAND YOU ARE LIVING. BUT AS FOR ME AND MY HOUSEHOLD, WE WILL SERVE THE LORD."
JOSHUA 24:15

"NO ONE CAN SERVE TWO MASTERS. EITHER HE WILL HATE THE ONE AND LOVE THE OTHER, OR HE WILL BE DEVOTED TO THE ONE AND DESPISE THE OTHER.'"
MATTHEW 6:24

We've talked about the principle of bad choice, bad conse-quence. Because we've had a lifetime to see that lived out, you and I know that is true. But our kids somehow think that if they can avoid instant consequences, maybe they've dodged that bullet. Maybe there won't be consequences. Maybe they got away with it, after all. The here and now seems so very real when compared to the far away land of tomorrow and consequences. We need a concrete example of what consequences are and how they work.

"Hey Daniel, look what I have here. It's something you love — a huge Hershey's chocolate bar! Doesn't it look great?

"I have a choice for you. I'm getting ready to make dinner in a few minutes. I was thinking of using this Hershey bar and making your absolute favorite dessert in the whole world — a Hershey bar pie. You may choose. Do you want to eat the Hershey bar now or do you want me to make a pie with it? I only have one chocolate bar so you have to choose one or the other. To choose one is to give up the possibility of the other. Think about which one you want to choose while you and I talk about it for a minute.

"I know it may sound silly, but life is a lot like having to choose between this Hershey and the pie. There was an old saying that said, 'You can't have your cake and eat it, too.' You can either eat it or you can still have it. But if you want to have it, you can't eat it. If you want to eat it, you can't still have it.

Learn the power of consequences now ... lest you face the consequences later

"Here's the issue. You do get to choose. You can choose your actions or you can choose your consequences, but you can't choose both. If you choose your action, like eating the Hershey bar, then you lose the right to choose the consequence. The Hershey bar is gone; you can no longer choose to make it into a pie later. If you want to choose the consequence, still having the Hershey bar to make into a pie later, then you gave up the right to choose the action. You cannot eat the Hershey bar now.

"If you choose your actions, the consequences will follow. You no longer have the right to choose them. They are dictated by the actions you chose. If you want to choose the consequences, then the actions are a given. They are dictated by the consequences you have chosen. I can't have my Hershey bar and eat it, too.

"Whether you choose a Hershey bar now or a pie later is not a big deal, but can you see the application for real life? If you don't want to get in trouble for being sassy or talking back (a consequence), then you must speak respectfully to everyone around you

154

(a choice). If you want to get good grades in school (a consequence), then you must study every day (a choice). If you want to still be pure on your wedding day (a consequence), then you must avoid any activity that might lead to sexual temptation now (a choice). If you choose to abstain from drinking alcohol while you are underage (a choice), you will never have to worry about being arrested for underage drinking or driving under the influence (a consequence). If you choose not to gossip or talk unkindly about any of your friends (a choice), then you will not need to worry about them getting mad at you and losing a friendship over what you said (a consequence).

"Do you see how consistent the principle is? We can choose either our actions, or we can choose our consequences, but we cannot choose both.

"How does this apply personally to you? Tell me one consequence that you know you want to have in your life. What actions must happen for you to actually see that consequence? What one action do you really want to see in your life? What will the consequence of that action be? Is there some way that you want me to help you in either one of those areas?

"Let's agree to hold each other accountable here. We'll remind each other that although we would love to be able to choose both, we can't. Let's pray that God will give us the grace to think long-term and to choose wisely.

"Now, which will it be? Shall we eat the Hershey bar or make it into a pie for dinner tonight?"

Date #47

Dating, American Style

"BE DEVOTED TO ONE ANOTHER IN BROTHERLY LOVE.
HONOR ONE ANOTHER ABOVE YOURSELVES."
ROMANS 12:10

For some of us, dating and the high school/college era are some of our fondest memories. Others live in fear of how they will explain it should their children ever ask them about their dating lives. Either way, we want to be deliberate in what we teach our kids about their relationships with the opposite sex. We want them to learn to be a blessing to everyone around them, whether male or female, whether a short term relationship or a lifelong one.

"Joel, I was watching Mike in church on Sunday and he looks so sad! It just breaks my heart to see him so discouraged. Are he and Katie still not speaking to each other? I'm so sorry. You know, any time we can learn from someone else's sufferings, it's a cheap way to learn a lesson. I think God has a lesson in this for us.

"Do you remember when we first got our puppy, Mandy? When she had an 'accident' on the carpet in the living room, it was really hard to housebreak her and convince her to wait until someone let her out to go to the bathroom. The reason why is that she had almost instantly formed a habit. And a habit is a hard thing to break.

"When we talk about Mandy and housebreaking, we're talking about a physical habit. But a habit of the heart is just as hard, maybe even harder, to break. I'm afraid that dating, American style, is training a habit of the heart that is going to hurt a lot of people you know. It is actually the perfect training for divorce!

"I know that sounds harsh, but I want you to keep in mind the habit of the heart concept while I describe the typical scenario at a middle school or high school. 'Tom' picks out a girl who he thinks is cute. He asks her out. They continue going out until she no longer makes him feel good about himself or happy. He then breaks up with her and looks for another girl who makes him feel good. Again, he dates her until she no longer makes him feel good or happy. So he breaks up with her and might even decide not to date again for awhile. He's not even looking; then

Dating, American style, is the perfect training for divorce.

a cute new girl transfers into his Spanish class and makes his heart flutter. She makes him feel so happy when he's with her that he decides to ask her out … and here we go again. Can you guess what Tom will do when this new girl no longer makes him 'feel' anything different?

"Can you see how he has trained his heart? He sticks with a relationship until it no longer serves his purposes, no longer makes him feel good, then he ends it. What will happen to Tom when he, as a young married man, looks over at his new bride and realizes that she doesn't make him happy? If he has trained his heart to give up when a relationship is less than perfect, can you see how he has set himself up for divorce? No human relationship ever makes us happy all of the time. It doesn't matter whether it's because we see their self-centeredness or our own, some ugly feelings will eventually surface. Emotions are cyclical; no one feels good about any relationship all of the time. Tom's training will make it harder for him to stick it out and work through his problems; there's nothing in his past relationships that taught him that habit of the heart.

"Here is my caution to you, Joel. What do you think Tom's relationships will be like with any of his ex-girlfriends? You're right; not very good. There's no such thing as going back to 'just being friends.' As good as it sounds; it's not usually emotionally possible for both people. You have some really wonderful female friends in your life. To choose to 'date' any of them is, most likely, to choose to end the friendship. You're not likely to get married in the next few years, so be cautious when crossing that line. Get to know all of the amazing Christian female friends God has given you. Be careful as you set 'habits of the heart' as it relates to dating.

"Romans 12:10 tells us to, 'Be devoted to one another in brotherly love. Consider one another above yourselves.' All relationships are meant to be redemptive in some way. If it's someone you're excited about getting to know, it's obvious you think highly of her. The goal is to protect the relationship, to serve the other person and not yourself.

"There is an added benefit to pursuing relationships this way. It will protect you in the long run. I know it sounds corny, but the older you get, the smaller the world seems. You will, most likely, walk into a young married Sunday School class someday, and the teacher's wife will be someone you were interested in during college. If you conducted yourself in a manner that left no regrets, you will be able to be excited about sitting next to them on the front row and comparing what God has done in your lives since you saw each other. If it ended poorly, it's going to be awkward for everyone involved.

"The goal here is to be cautious of two things: that the habits of the heart that we train are ones that honor both the Lord and those around us and that the way we treat others leaves us with regret-free relationships. I'll be praying for you son — that God will help you to develop relational habits that honor Him and those around you. Thanks for listening to me. I love you. I'm proud of the fact that you're trying to handle your relationships with integrity. You're going to be an amazing husband and father someday!"

Date #48

Mirror, Mirror on the Wall

"BE VERY CAREFUL, THEN, HOW YOU LIVE — NOT AS
UNWISE, BUT AS WISE, MAKING THE MOST OF EVERY
OPPORTUNITY, BECAUSE THE DAYS ARE EVIL."
EPHESIANS 5:15

"TEACH US TO NUMBER OUR DAYS ARIGHT, THAT WE
MAY GAIN A HEART OF WISDOM."
PSALM 90:12

Mrs. Mario N. Zandstra. Lynelle Zandstra. Mrs. Lynelle Zandstra. Do you remember that first crush? The one where you scribbled your "new" name on your notebook paper while you were supposed to be paying attention in class? Or, you imagined how jealous all of your buddies would be when you walked in with her on your arm? Although it's a natural part of growing up, we want our teens to focus more on who they are becoming than on who they are catching!

"Laura, can we go out to dinner tonight? Dad has offered to keep the little kids so that you and I can have some 'girl time.' You may pick any restaurant you want — it's your choice! We have been so busy lately that I haven't gotten much time with you and I really miss you. Let's be ready to leave at 6:30. Can you have most of your homework finished by then? Good. It's a date."

Later, at the restaurant.

"I can't even begin to tell you how proud of you I am, Laura. You are becoming an absolutely beautiful young lady! I think you are amazing.

"I have a gift for you tonight. It's a purity journal. Open the front cover and you'll see a note that I wrote you. It talks about how proud of you I am and how I'm looking forward to this next stage of life with you.

"I want you to turn the page and open it to the first blank page. I'm going to give you about five minutes to do something. I want you to list everything you can think of that you want in a husband. Everything! I want you to tell me what he will be like, look like, act like, think about, get excited about. I want to know what his sense of humor will be like and what his heart will be like. I'll give you about five minutes to compile a list of everything you can think of."

Focus on becoming, not on catching.

Five minutes later.

"May I look at your list? Why don't you read it out loud to me? Wow! That is an amazing man of God you've described. You did a great job of describing what a real man after God's own heart will look like! What a great vision for what you want in a husband. He is a real Prince Charming.

"Now I have a question. When this Prince Charming decides to get married, what will his princess look like? Describe for me what kind of princess this prince will want to marry. I'll give you about five minutes again."

Five minutes later.

"It's been five minutes. May I look at your list again? Wow! What an amazing woman of God you've described. You're right; Prince Charming would be honored to have her as his bride.

"The world will force you to make a decision soon, darling. Everything in our culture will try to convince you to focus on catching this — Prince Charming. What I want to help you focus on is becoming this — the princess. You will have to make a choice between focusing on *catching* or *becoming*.

"God wants you to make the most of every opportunity, to focus on becoming more Godly, so that you are ready when and if He brings someone into your life. Here is a little gift to help remind you of what you're trying to do. It's a tie (or a hair ribbon for a young man). You can hang it on your desk or bathroom mirror or wherever you choose. Every time you see it, it will remind you of two things. First, it will remind you to pray for your prince every day — that God will do a great and mighty work in and through Him, getting him ready for whatever He calls him to do. Secondly, it will remind you to make the most of every day, to focus on becoming rather than catching. Purity is more than just what you do; it is who you are.

"I am so proud of who you are becoming, sweetie. You are becoming more conformed to the image of Christ every day, and I'm so glad that God gave you to me. I love you."

Date #49

A Theology of Sex

"BUT AMONG YOU THERE MUST NOT BE EVEN A HINT OF
SEXUAL IMMORALITY, OR OF ANY KIND OF IMPURITY, OR
OF GREED, BECAUSE THESE ARE IMPROPER FOR GOD'S
HOLY PEOPLE."
EPHESIANS 5:3

"LIVE AS CHILDREN OF LIGHT (FOR THE FRUIT OF THE
LIGHT CONSISTS IN ALL GOODNESS, RIGHTEOUSNESS
AND TRUTH) AND FIND OUT WHAT PLEASES THE LORD."
EPHESIANS 5:8-10

OK, I got your attention just by the title of this section, didn't I? Very few of us would argue the fact that we have a problem with passion in our culture. Mario and I were speaking at a marriage conference in a large town and had slipped out to a deli to grab a sandwich for lunch. As we ate, I glanced at a local campus newspaper. An article on the front page caught my eye. It was a synopsis of the results of a recent survey on campus, claiming that 30 percent of all seniors at the university had experimented with either homosexuality or bisexuality by the time they were seniors. Horrified yet?

I recently heard a gentleman speak on internet pornography. He quoted the following statistics:

500,000 pages of new internet pornography are added every year

30 percent of all of those pages are aimed at children

The average age of first exposure to internet pornography in the U.S. is between the ages of 9 and 11.

If there were an epidemic raging across our country, we would be the first to rush out and immunize our kids. There is an epidemic; it's called sexual permissiveness. It says that anything goes, sexually. We MUST protect our children by giving them a theology of sex. They need to learn to be the same person on Friday night that they are on Sunday morning.

Mario is fond of saying that, "Da Nile is more than a river in Egypt; it's my wife's middle name." I hate even having to think about this stuff as it relates to my kids. But we've got to protect them by preparing them. We can teach them about passion or the world will do it for us.

"Boys, let's do something fun tonight. Why don't you go build a fire out in the fire pit in the backyard? While you boys do that, I'll go buy marshmallow, graham crackers, and Hershey bars. As soon as you have a roaring fire, we'll make s'mores and sit out there and enjoy the stars. I'll be back with the supplies in 30 minutes. I'll meet you at the fire pit."

A solid theology of sex is vital in today's day and age.

When the fire is raging.

"This is a really great fire, guys. Good job. Don't the s'mores taste great? But it's getting kind of late and we need to move inside to keep an eye on the little ones. I really hate to not get to sit by the fire any longer, though. It has really been enjoyable.

"I have a solution. Why don't we just move the fire inside? Let's rebuild it in the middle of the living room. Joel, you bring the firewood, and Will, you bring the lighter fluid and some kindling. What do you mean, 'That would be crazy?' We just said how good the fire is. Why shouldn't we move it inside?

"You are absolutely right, guys. The problem is not with the fire at all. A fire is a good thing. The problem is with the proposed placement. A fire in the living room would be a destructive thing. It is, quite simply, in the wrong place. We would burn our house down because we didn't consider the proper placement.

"Our culture tells us that it's OK to build a fire anywhere and you won't get burned. That is pretty naïve, isn't it? We know the truth, though. The place where you build the fire is all important. The fire that I'm talking about is sexuality. It was created by God and it is good. But only in the right place; it's meant for marriage alone. Built anywhere else, it will burn down a house or a relationship. In movies, magazines, internet, billboards, television shows, and books, our culture tells us that it doesn't matter where we build a fire. Just because they say it doesn't make it true. A lie is a lie no matter how many people repeat it.

"The next time you hear someone talking about sex outside of marriage, I want you to remember this fire, and how it is a good thing when it's in the proper place. Any place else, it is an incredibly destructive force. The problem is not with the fire, it's with the place."

Date #50

A Scary World

"FOR THE EARTH WILL BE FILLED WITH THE KNOWLEDGE OF THE GLORY OF THE LORD, AS THE WATERS COVER THE SEA."
HABAKKUK 2:14

"IN THIS WORLD YOU WILL HAVE TROUBLE. BUT TAKE HEART! I HAVE OVERCOME THE WORLD."
JOHN 16:33B

"IS ANY ONE OF YOU IN TROUBLE? HE SHOULD PRAY. THE PRAYER OF A RIGHTEOUS MAN IS POWERFUL AND EFFEC-TIVE."
JAMES 5:13A & 16B

Between wars, genocide, famines, and other man-made disasters, no one has trouble believing John 16:33, *"In this world you will have trouble."* Just watching the news or reading the newspaper can be a scary thing. It would be an easy, and an understandable thing, to want to hide, but is that the Christian response? What do we teach our children about all of the suffering around us? How do we teach them to engage a culture gone berserk?

The answer lies in the last part of Jesus' quote in John 16:33, *"But take heart. I have overcome the world."* That is our only hope; let's teach our kids to appropriate it.

"Kids, we're going to start something new at breakfast this week. We're going to look at the newspaper together every morning. The major world events are usually on the front page. Let's take a look at the headlines. It's pretty grim, isn't it? Unfortunately, the major world events are mostly conflicts and disasters. It is easy to get discouraged when we look at them. It looks like there's no way man can ever solve all of these dilemmas. And you know what, we can't. But listen to Jesus' words to us in John 16:33. He says, *'In this world you will have trouble. But take heart. I have overcome the world.'*

It's easy to get discouraged when you look at the world around you ... but we must look to God and be encouraged!

"Now we have gone from discouraging to encouraging. Man is responsible for most of these problems and could never solve them all. But Jesus has promised that He will overcome them all.

"So what should be our response to all of these problems? Let's look at James 5:13 & 16, *"Is any one of you in trouble? He should pray. The prayer of a righteous man is powerful and effective."* I would say that we are clearly in trouble in this world. So our response should be what? That's right — prayer.

"That's what we want to do for just a few minutes every morning at breakfast. We'll start by looking at the headlines and talking about what the issue is. Why are they fighting? What are they fighting about? What caused this famine or drought? Why is this policy or law that they are debating such a big deal? We might even have to do some research in order to understand some of these issues. Then we'll be able to pray more knowledgably.

"We'll pray that God will intervene in each of these situations and resolve them in a way that brings glory to Himself. And we'll thank Him that although these things look unsolvable, He has overcome the world. That means we don't need to worry; we need to pray and be thankful. Aren't you glad we serve a sovereign God? I sure am!

"Let's start praying for the world around us today. Who wants to run out to the mailbox and bring in the newspaper? We'll pray with Habakkuk that, *'The earth will be filled with the knowledge of the glory of the Lord, as the water fills the sea!'* What a great prayer. Thanks for doing this with me, guys."

Date #51

Decorating a Hotel Room

"SO WE FIX OUR EYES NOT ON WHAT IS SEEN, BUT ON WHAT IS UNSEEN. FOR WHAT IS SEEN IS TEMPORARY, BUT WHAT IS UNSEEN IS ETERNAL."
II CORINTHIANS 4:18

If you're anywhere near my age, you may remember a commercial a few years ago for a brokerage house. As the very wise, very successful looking broker began to offer his advice to the young couple, every conversation in the room ceased. In the following hush, the entire room leaned visibly forward, hanging on his every word of advice. His financial advice, while important today, will be the chaff of tomorrow. We have something much greater to offer our kids — advice that effects their eternity.

Staying in a hotel is an absolute treat for my kids. For some unknown reason, they love everything about it. The hotel stay itself is reason enough for rejoicing in their world, but if we find one that has an indoor pool and hot tub, it's as good as it gets!

We don't, though, tend to stay in a lot of hotels. The reason? Money. Because there are nine of us, we are against fire code in one

room. We have to rent two rooms in order to meet legal require-
ments. The cost of one room seems high in itself; now double it for
two rooms and you'll see why we stay in few hotels.

On this night, though, we were actually going to stay in a
hotel. After driving 10 hours that day, we found a hotel with two
adjoining available rooms. To my kids' delight, the hotel had an
indoor pool and hot tub! With total glee, they threw on their swimming suits and raced down to the pool. Splashing, jumping, and
squealing, they moved back and forth between cannon-balls into
the pool and soaking tired little bodies in the hot tub.

Eventually, the dreaded time came. Closing time for the
pool. Sadly they trooped, single file and silent so as not to awaken
sleeping neighbors, back to our rooms. Once there, teeth brushed
and pajama clad, they announced in one voice, "We're starving!"
Not about to get back into the car again that day, Mario went in
search of food.

Can you imagine their delight, when, five minutes later,
Mario returned with cans of Dr Pepper, bags of M&M's, and
Doritos? Since this was not a big enough hotel to have its own
restaurant, the only option had been the vending machines in the
hall. The kids dove into the junk food with reckless abandon.

The food frenzy over, they began to look for late night activ-
ities. My two little gymnasts soon discovered that the beds were
close enough together that they could actually do somersaults and
back flips from one bed to another. Although we have strict rules
against jumping on beds at home, the next 10 minutes was spent in
a carefully supervised Somersault Olympics, designed to burn off
the last remaining energy of the day.

As we began to unwind and get ready to collapse into bed,
one of the younger children walked over and switched on the TV.
It was just like the broker commercial; absolute silence followed.
Perhaps I should say, "delighted" silence. We live too far out of town
for cable television. Satellite never seemed worth the money, so we
were left with three very fuzzy local stations that were rarely worth
watching.

After about a 30 second silence, Daniel said, "Oh, wow!
Mom, Dad, did you know that Disney has its own channel?"

Convinced that this really is as good as it gets, they settled down into their beds to watch 30 minutes of Goofy and Mickey Mouse cartoons as they drifted happily off to sleep.

The next Sunday night, now returned home from our trip, we prepared to light the second candle of our annual advent wreath.

"Kids, tonight is the candle of hotel keys," I said as I held up the card from the hotel.

"No, Mom, I'm pretty sure it is the candle of promise," Hannah responded.

"She's right. I don't remember anything about hotel cards," Mary Claire added.

"You're right. Usually it would be promise, but tonight we're going to change things a little bit and instead have the candle of hotel key cards," I answered.

"Do you remember how much fun we had at that hotel last week?" I asked. "We swam in the pool and the hot tub until it closed. We ate M&M's and Doritos and drank Dr Pepper. We jumped on the beds until we were worn out and we watched the Disney channel as we went to bed. It was a great night, wasn't it?"

They all agreed that it had been one of the most fun nights of the whole year.

"Then I have a proposition for you. If it was one of the most fun nights of the whole year, I vote we do something about it. The banks are closed because it's Sunday, but when they reopen tomorrow, I vote that we go take all of the money out of all seven of your savings accounts. Then let's go back and really deck out that hotel room!

"Let's get rid of that little bitty refrigerator and put in side-by-side subzero refrigerators. And let's fill them with Dr Peppers and M&M's! Then let's get rid of that little hotel room TV and put in a big screen TV with surround-sound speakers. Let's throw away the bedspreads they had and put down comforters on all of the beds so that they will be even more comfortable for jumping.

"What do you think?" I asked. "Are you in?"

A long, awkward silence followed. Finally, Daniel, who was 6 at the time, raised his hand and spoke up. "Mom, I could be wrong here, but I don't think that would be a very good idea," he hesitantly suggested.

"Why not?" I demanded.

"Because, Mom, as fun as that night at the hotel was, that hotel is not our home. We were only passing through."

"You're right, darling. I think you've got it. It would be pretty silly to choose to decorate a hotel room, wouldn't it? We know we're only there for a short amount of time and that's not where we want to put our money, our time, or our hearts. It would be an absolute waste. None of us would do that.

"But we make that decision every day of our lives. II Corinthians 4:18 tells us that, 'We fix our eyes not on what is seen, but on what is unseen. For what is seen is temporary, but what is unseen is eternal.' The book of Hebrews calls us 'aliens' and 'strangers' and says that we are only passing through this world.

"This world is not our real, permanent home. Heaven is. We would never seriously consider decorating a hotel room. We want to invest in that which is real and permanent and eternal. Let's do the same thing with our lives. Let's ask God to give us the grace, as a family, to invest in that which is eternal.

This world is not our real, permanent home. Heaven is.

"I asked the man at the hotel desk if I could have nine cards. I bought nine crosses, tied ribbons through them and glued them to the cards. There is one of these for each of us. The big kids can hang them from their rear-view mirrors in their cars. The younger ones can hang them in your bathrooms or use them for Bible bookmarks. But we want these keys with crosses to remind us that we make a choice every day. We choose to either decorate a hotel room or invest in eternity.

"Let's commit, as a family, to encourage each other not to decorate that hotel room. Can we do that? I love you guys and I'm glad you're mine!"

For Every Parent

As a parent, pray this with me: "Lord God, Almighty, would you please give us the grace to remember not to decorate a hotel room? Everything in our culture encourages us to fill up on chips and not even be hungry for the banquet that you have provided us in yourself. Forgive us for being so easily satisfied with chips. Please give us an insatiable craving for you. Let us never be satisfied with the false pleasures the world has to offer, but only to hunger after real, eternal treasure. Lord, give us lives, as parents, that are worthy of being imitated, because we know they will be. Let our kids see in us that which we want to see in them. Father, we all tend to think, on our death beds, of the legacy that we leave behind. But we know that's too late. Help us to consider, today, the legacy we leave. Help us leave a legacy of a life invested in that which is truly eternal. Show us ways to live out that which we believe. Give us the grace to pass on a life-changing spiritual heritage."

A Final Prayer

Now to Him who is able to do immeasurably more than all we ask or imagine, according to his power that is at work within us, to him be glory in the church and in Christ Jesus throughout all generations, forever and ever! Amen.

To find out more about Lynelle Zandstra and her ministry, to order additional resources, or to inquire about booking her to speak at your event, contact Lynelle directly at:

www.LynelleZandstra.com

Choose Words, Choose Life